Best-selling author, philosopher, economist, entrepreneur, poet and musician, Elio D'Anna is the writer of the international best-seller 'School for Gods' and the founder and president of the European School of Economics.

A music industry pioneer and a visionary entrepreneur, Elio's organisations are world leaders in a wide ranging of sectors, from education, to hospitality, to entertainment and technology.

A renowned international speaker for conferences and seminars all over the world, he advances the principles of the 'Inner Economy' as the only means to give rise to a new global economic paradigm. Through his foundation and philanthropic initiatives, he organises annual fundraising events aimed at fostering research and expanding access to education for deserving students across the world.

*"To you, I am speaking.
To you, who read, I am speaking. To you, who, for many years, have wandered in a maze of texts searching for something that would give meaning to a life without meaning.*

"I am you. I am the reality that vibrates inside while you read me—nourishment for what you are and the power to remove what you are not.

"My message, if you are strong enough to contain it, will set you free from superstitions, false ideas and second-hand knowledge that are the useless materials that you have collected over many years of neglect. If you are strong enough to free yourself of it, then my word will take root, and with it, a new life."

The Dreamer

Elio D'Anna

THE TECHNOLOGY OF THE DREAMER

AUSTIN MACAULEY PUBLISHERS™
LONDON • CAMBRIDGE • NEW YORK • SHARJAH

Copyright © Elio D'Anna (2020)

The right of Elio D'Anna to be identified as author of this work has been asserted by him in accordance with section 77 and 78 of the Copyright, Designs and Patents Act 1988.

All rights reserved. No part of this publication may be reproduced, stored in a retrieval system or transmitted in any form or by any means, electronic, mechanical, photocopying, recording or otherwise, without the prior permission of the publishers.

Any person who commits any unauthorised act in relation to this publication may be liable to criminal prosecution and civil claims for damages.

A CIP catalogue record for this title is available from the British Library.

ISBN 9781788236782 (Paperback)
ISBN 9781528953733 (ePub e-book)

www.austinmacauley.com

First Published (2020)
Austin Macauley Publishers Ltd
25 Canada Square
Canary Wharf
London
E14 5LQ

Table of Contents

Chapter I — 15

The Art of Dreaming — 15
Identification Is Slavery — 27
At the Mercy of Lesser Gods — 36

Chapter II — 45

Dreaming and Desire — 45
Dream if You Want to Change — 60
Victim of the Visible — 70
The Laws of the Deuteronomy — 77

Chapter III — 81

The Art of Acting — 81
Acting Is Surrender — 95
The Unity That Pulses — 96
The Chant of Humanity — 97
Believing Without Believing — 102
Win It Before It Happens — 113
The Art of Acting at the Times of Lupelius — 115
To Be Is to Not Be — 116

Chapter IV — 119

No War Within, No War Without — 119
What's 'Fair' and What's 'Unfair' — 136
The Titanic Task — 151
The Perfect Joy — 152
You Should Only Ever Win — 162
Freedom or Oblivion — 169

Chapter V — 171

The Others — 171
The Individual and the Mass — 191
Out of the Crowd — 205

Chapter VI — 207

Being and Having — 207
On the Edge of the Abyss — 222

The Will	225
Fearlessness	229
The Second Education	239
Thoughtlessness	242
Money Is a Rubber Band	244
This Is Economics	245
The Fleeting Moment	248
Integrity in Action	251
The 'Yes' Attitude	254

Chapter VII — **257**

The Body	257
The World Is the Symptom	267
The Cult of Death	273
Fasting	277
Voluntary Death	286

Chapter VIII — **299**

Timelessness	299
Time-Worshippers	311
Conscious Suffering	321
The Kingdom of Now	326

The Fairy-tale of Your Own — **327**

Birth and Death — **327**

I've been you a thousand times.
You will be me once and forever.

This Book
The Non-Teaching of the Dreamer

This book is you,
With all your doubts and certainties,
Truths and lies, fears and love.

You are, at the same time, the writer and the reader,
The ordinary and the remarkable...

The Dreamer and the dreamed.

This book is for those who are disappointed with their ordinary life and are looking for something they have lost and forgotten for so long; something special.

This book is for those who want to abandon all forms of lying.

This book is about your inner states and deals with your inner reactions to the others and to the outer world; here you will learn to distinguish between yourself and the external, between cause and effect, between time and timelessness—between what is real and what is not.

In a world where all revolutions have failed, and the many attempts to change the violent and reactive nature of man have been revealed to be useless, the 'Non-Teaching' of the Dreamer presents itself as the only way to transform events and circumstances, past and future, history and destiny at will.

The Dreamer...

In this moment, he is here, in front of you and yet you cannot see him.

He lives amongst you, he walks amongst you, and yet he remains invisible to you, whom, having not yet abandoned your personal history, feel not the need for a commitment to reach a higher level of understanding.

A visionary being, a man of integrity; the Dreamer embodies within himself something subversive, unexpected and impossible to grasp; something that violates the ordinary course of things. He is free from any sort of role, description, influence or constraint, both within and without. He appears and disappears at will, taking on any role in the world of events that He is required to play.

But do not dare to put the Dreamer into your senseless line-up of gurus and masters, or compare his 'non-teaching' to that formless mass of esotericism, spirituality, religion and philosophy. Any attempt to give a form to or describe the Dreamer, to try to rationalise His behaviour, to understand His psychology, to then include it among the philosophical currents of the past or describe it as eclectic shamanism, is useless and in vain.

Only those who have a real dream can access the inaccessible, and only those who have eyes to see will one day be able to see the Dreamer and know that he is the real doer.

It is, therefore, time to ignore all teachings, ideologies, disciplines, books, ideas, both your own and those of others; all spoken or written words and finally plunge into the depths of your being to find your own uniqueness and power. It is time to understand that knowledge is limitation, a barrier to freedom, that knowledge is only a pale description of what reality is, and as such, it only closes off your intuition and happiness and prevents you from going beyond.

The Non-Teaching of the Dreamer is here to eliminate more than to add on. To eliminate old structures, rusted concepts, obsolete ideas, to abandon preconceived notions, false sentiments, imaginary fears and identification, to destroy negative emotions, destructive thoughts and the very idea that has been rooted in every man since childhood: *the inevitability of death.*

The 'Work' announced by the Dreamer, is first of all, a work of transformation of thought; from a conflict-ridden consciousness to an inner state of integrity, from an empirical, reactive man to an intuitive, creative being. His principles and ideas are the result of long years of self-study and enquiries. They deal with the most important subject of study—oneself, and are aimed at the realisation that the world is your own projection—that the world is how you dream it.

Because of this, the Dreamer uses the theatre of life to raise your intelligence and aliveness. He uses history, religions, politics and all forms of business and educational systems; communication, media, every human and natural disasters and everything you believe to be coming from the world outside, for the sole purpose of awakening you—to show you that you, yourself, are the source of all things.

'The world is such because you are such'

With this message, so simple and yet so revolutionary, the Dreamer brings you a very powerful *technology,* capable of guiding you into the depths of your drowsiness to bring you face to face with your doubts, fears, complaints and anxieties. It is a journey into all that which is unpleasant, a journey to abandon your dearest possession, something that you love more than your life and which is the very cause of your every failure: *your own suffering.*

With the Dreamer, you enter into an uncharted territory. His words will mercilessly enter into the innermost recesses of your being with the precision of a surgeon until your vision will be turned upside down, and with it all that you have believed to be your world, your life.

Here you don't have any road maps. You have nothing from the past to guide and direct you, and you will have no images of the future when venturing into the unknown. You have to be fluid and impeccable, able to shift in an instant, holding on to no experience, no knowledge, no expectation and just sharing with Him, the same victory over death, the same beauty, the same passion for life.

The inner journey is a very hard, dangerous task, and only those who have the courage to leave behind their mediocrity and their meaningless life may embark upon it.

You will find within yourself mountains, oceans, deserts, forests, cliffs and abysses to overcome; wild beasts, horrible monsters and impossible battles to win just like the most arduous, adventurous expeditions on earth.

It is a journey for only the few among few who have realised that their life has to change dramatically, and more than anything, their way of dreaming; and only few among those few, will succeed.

To stop identifying with the description of the world is the aim of the Non-Teaching. That's why the Dreamer will become your worst enemy—the enemy of your wrong ideas and false knowledge that you have cultivated for so long. By following the Dreamer, your vanity and presumption will be constantly attacked and beaten to death until you either understand and continue your path towards integrity, or get hurt in your false pride and leave in indignation.

But never forget that the answers given by the Dreamer are very personal and cannot be meant for everybody. They respond to the questioner's inner state of responsibility and freedom and take strictly in consideration his/her own level of understanding.

The Dreamer is dreaming an individual revolution; a world without religions, without politics; a world that eliminates every form of institution, every form of division and every fear. It is the advent of a new man, beyond imagination, inconceivable for those whose feet are cemented in the past, whose hands are full of compromise.

In this journey, memory and imagination, thoughts and emotions will disappear, cancelling the grimace of their technologies—obsolete instruments of a lost humanity.

Only intuition and dream will remain. These are the new technologies to create and to know.

The non-teaching of the Dreamer reveals the secret of all secrets; here you will enter deep into your heart and find what you have been looking for…

This is not the end of the world,
It is the end of a story, of a description.

It is no longer time to suffer, nor time to die.
It's time to live a new dream, a new world, a new life!

Chapter I
The Art of Dreaming

*All comes from within,
If you could understand this, all fears would disappear, and when all fears are gone, you will have a new name: God*

Dreaming is the Supreme Art of the Gods.
Ordinary man cannot dream but can only be dreamed.

All we see and touch, all we perceive, the skyscrapers of finance, the pyramids of industry, the discoveries and achievements of science and technology, all we call 'reality', is nothing but the projection of an inner invisible world, a world of ideas and values that runs vertically to the plane of our existence: the world of being.

The physical world, the entire universe with its apparent infinity, has never existed before or after this timeless instant, and you yourself are the sole author, actor and audience of this magnificent, multi-coloured musical that you call life.

You are the Dreamer.

And whatever events, upheavals or miracles take place in the outer world, they first have to occur in your body; there, where your very dream lies.

But be careful with mistaking dreaming as the product of an oneiric activity; it does not occur whilst you sleep.

Dreaming means 'doing'. It is a state of freedom, a psychological condition of absence of fear, anxiety, doubts and negative emotions.

Dreaming means to be right 'now' what you wish to become.

Dreaming is that creative power which
lies hidden within you.
Dreaming is the root of all existence and of what
gives life to the entire universe.
Dreaming is an inner revolution which will turn
your reality completely upside-down.
Dreaming is the impeccable, inner transformation
of a self-making god.

You have experimented with this creation as a child. You wanted to test your ability to transform the world and so you tried to exercise your power to move objects outside of yourself: a pen on the table, the glance of a person close by, the invitation of a friend. You sought a space within yourself and called this event into being. It's a marvellous game that now has to be played 'seriously'. Seriously means that it must come from this stillness, that it touches something real within you transforming the world instantly.

Contrary to the years and layers of second-hand education, false ideas, conditioning and programming that have cemented in you the firm belief that you are just one amongst billions, insignificant and powerless in front of the world's events, it is in reality all up to you—you're dreaming and creating reality, whether good or bad, at this very moment. Everything is in your hands. Everything depends upon you. Everything has the meaning that you give to it.

You are the seed of the universe.

And without giving attention to the seed, the universe degrades and disappears. So, let life becomes a masterpiece! Only you can do it. Only now.

As impossible as it might be for you to fathom, all your life is happening right now; from the atom to God, there is nothing outside of this instant. What you are right now radiates in all directions and determines what you already have been and always will be.

Therefore, whatever you have done up to now doesn't matter. It doesn't influence at all what you're going to do, because what you believe you have been living has never really happened; your personal history begins in this very instant. Your past has never existed but in your imagination.

If you learn how 'to be' permanently in the 'here now', you not only will be in charge of your life, but the entire world will depend on your command.

Remember! You can be, know, do and create only in the now.

But everyone wrongly considers his or her personal memory as the most real thing they possess, and their own past as the root of their life; people would and could never be able to renounce this idea. However, our memory is deceitful; it is programmed now, and occurs in this very instant—just as the imagination of the future.

We do not see the world as it is but as we think it is, through the lenses of our *belief system;* our convictions create in this very moment all that we think is our past and our future. In it, there is the programming of all that has been and all that will be.

So, if you want to change your life, just remember yourself—have yourself present all the time, understand that everything that you are now, you have always been and will always be—past and future; and the secret hidden in your own being will be revealed and spread out in all directions.

What is this secret?

Simple; that you are all that is great, beautiful and powerful, and at the same time, you are nothing, have nothing, can do nothing; yet all comes out of you—the source is you, the root, the very cause of all is you.

This inner realisation, that everything comes from within and has to have your own consent to manifest, makes all the events and circumstances happen only for your advantage and growth.

On the contrary, if you believe that your world is an entity living outside yourself, you, like billions of people, in eons of time, will have to go through all troubles and difficulties, aging and disease, to one day understand that you are the very one who emanates this world that you believe to be external.

So, go back to yourself, look at yourself, search within, focus all your attention and dedicate all your efforts to raise the boundaries of your Dream. Dare to dive into the inaccessible, dare to touch the invisible and realise that reality will follow as a shadow to the object that casts it.

The dream is a plan that happens in absence of time in eternity, in a vertical time—in this very moment. By giving attention to the dream, to your living, feeling and thinking, you free yourself and go beyond and your false persona with its addictions and obsessions, memories and habits, lies and contradictions will dissolve.

Do not ask how it happens, it cannot be explained. What really matters is to enter in yourself with sincerity and earnestness—to be aware of your being as an ever-present fact; if you persevere in this action, there can be no failure in your life.

Remember! You cannot change the world without changing yourself, and when you are able to do that, you will realise that it is neither possible nor necessary to change others; because the only true revolution is your change.

The entire universe is only a pale shadow of your inner being; the more you realise that what surrounds you is happening nowhere else but within, the more power you will have for changing it.

The slightest change in your being moves mountains in the world of events.

You

If I am the Dreamer and creator of this world, why did I create so much trouble and suffering in it?

The Dreamer

Look upon this world as a movie and you will know why you create it as it is. If you watch a movie, you like to see in it a series of actions, adventures and dangers rather than something dull or boring. And this is the way you have to watch and enjoy your world: a spectacular, electronic play of light and shadows, good and evil, victory and defeat, joy and sorrow.

Everything is then the projection of your own being condensed into an appearance of characters and events.

You

If there is no time and no space between being and becoming, between dream and reality, how is it then, that what happens right now does not correspond at all to what I am dreaming of?

The Dreamer

Only a higher state of being, a vision from above, could make you realise that what you are experiencing right now is exactly the reality you are dreaming of.

Your life is such and couldn't be anything else because you never bring any change in your own dream, even if you're living hell! From where you are, dream and reality appear as two different worlds with no connection at all, but until you understand that the only way you can change the reality you are living in is to change your dream; to dream a new world—to create a new life, everything will remain the same.

Remember! Behind the apparent willingness to change your life, there is a greater determination to want to perpetuate it as it is.

You

But what about the world as a whole? How can we make it a better and fairer one for everyone?

The Dreamer

To change the world, you have to look no further than your own self. Most of you are conditioned by culture, by knowledge, by environment, by media, by food, clothes, money, politics, religion, sex and so on. Acknowledging this as your limitation and being aware of your inner slavery will make you free.

All conflicts, horrors, persecutions and injustice would come to an end, and with that, all disease, poverty and slavery would miraculously disappear from earth if you would earnestly inquire into yourself and fearlessly tackle the hidden, invisible generator of all crimes—your inner war.

You

Then, should we not try to improve the world we live in?

The Dreamer

It is not the world that you have to improve, but your way of looking—your inner attitude.

You can see the moon dancing on the restless waters of the lake but it is all appearance. The world has no existence apart from you.

You create it, you destroy it.
You improve it, you degrade it.

The world hangs on the thread of your being.
No being, no world.

All the events and experiences, senses and emotions, thoughts and images, the drama of opposites: attraction and aversion, war and peace, sickness and health, life and death, all happens in you yourself as the Dreamer and creator of all and everything.

Identification Is Slavery

When you realise that you are the one who creates and projects the reality you are living in, and that all depends upon you, a sense of loneliness comes and grips your being. You are alone, facing the abyss of yourself and the sense of responsibility that now weighs on your shoulders. Yet, in this moment of inner clarity, you begin to see the outside world as something that is profoundly part of yourself, you begin to see that the others are none other than the faithful materialisation of your inner states and moods, *and this will give you incredible power.*

Be here and now, and you will soon realise that the events occurring in your life are the final result of your inner states, and as such, whatever happens in your life has to have your inner approval, your inner consent for it to manifest. Sometimes unconsciously, we dream the most horrible nightmares, which, in their turn, become reality.

Any event happens the way it does, because you 'dream' it the way it happens.

If there is something you choose to experience in your life, do not desire it, but simply, be it! What you are now, the world is unmistakably mirroring and couldn't do otherwise; *the entire universe is impregnated with you.*

You are used to moving in the outside world in search of encounters and experiences, with the clear conviction that it is your hunting ground. When you meet others, when you go to work or to school, when you amuse yourself in whatever way pleases you, you never look at the world as your reflection but are instead convinced that there is indeed something to be taken from it—that something can come from outside of yourself. It is this very conviction that has cost you your integrity, and even your freedom.

You mark the passage of time in hours, months and years, and this is the first step of your journey through the self-created prison of identification. Only at the hour of reckoning do you realise that something doesn't add up, that time has tricked you.

This is why you are what you are, because you keep falling into this forgetfulness, and the world can't be anything but the faithful mirror of this amnesia. You shrink and drown in the lake of your own tears; you give in to the call of self-pity until you become small as an insect, lost in the crawling multitude of millions of other insects.

You believe to be intoxicated by the world around, but it is your very identification that creates an intoxicated world. Identification is toxicity, identification is poison—identification is slavery. Identification is simultaneously the very cause of all your troubles and misfortunes, as well as of all humanity's disasters and natural calamities.

You

You talk about becoming free from identification, and yet from the moment we are born, we are conditioned by everything around us, from family, to environment, to culture…
How can we then ever hope to get rid of our conditionings?

The Dreamer

When you are conscious of the fact that you are entirely conditioned or lost or identified with something, you have already become free of it.

You

For the majority of the world, happiness seems to be the true meaning and purpose of life, the whole aim of human existence.
What do you believe is the best way to achieve happiness?

The Dreamer

Don't look for happiness, look instead for unhappiness; it's easier, because apparently, unhappiness is governing your entire existence.

Instead of looking for truth, look for lies, look for pain, look for fear and you'll see that in trying to find them inside, you'll realise their total inexistence.

You

But why fear? Why pain? What is the reason for living in such a conflictual world so full of evil and disease, war and misery? Couldn't we live in a peaceful and harmonious world?

The Dreamer

This world is, for you, the school.
Without the world and its game of light and shadows, pain and pleasure, victory and defeat, life and death, it would take you thousands of years to achieve what can be accomplished in one short lifespan.
This world is of tremendous importance for you, because by going beyond it, you can realise your perfection.

'Whatever you ask, you will receive, and whatever you seek, you will find'.
You don't understand how powerful your imagination is! Your addiction to destructive thoughts and negative emotions is such that you cannot live without them. What you call reality, with all its wars and conflicts, is only a macabre distortion of your own fantasy; a gruesome play that you project for your own idle entertainment.

What you have to do now is to stop blaming the world for its horrors, violence and injustice, understand that what you believe to be objective is only a reflection of your own subjectivity and willingly take the whole matter on your own shoulders. It is your gloomy fantasy that has to be healed and not the world around. You have to realise that the only solution to all problems is to clear out your own vision, and focus all your attention on your inner integrity and perfection.

All wars would instantly be brought to an end if you could become aware of your conditioning; if you could earnestly inquire into yourself and get free of your inner fragmentation, of your inner misery, of your inner war. If you could dive within yourself, in stillness, secret and silence, you would reveal an energy so powerful that an all new dimension and a brand-new world will be instantly projected before you.

This is what real 'doing' is: real 'doing' is the ability to create the life you desire through the transformation of your inner chemistry without physical action.

Remember! There is nothing in the universe that is not 'you'. Therefore, dream only an 'impeccable you' and you will be entertained by a beautiful world.

The whole '*game*' is based on entering into the abyss of the unknown, remembering at the same time that there is no abyss at all. On entering into the forgotten innermost recesses of your own being, and touch what is really able to change the world.

You think you are the effect, the victim of a world that gives you a reality you do not like. But you are the creator. There is not an objective world established, the same for everyone. The world is as you dream it, and even what appears to be negative, destructive to you, is just the reflection of your conflictual inner being.

The world is such because you are such.

All this time, you've been mistaking the world for reality—exchanging a flat lifeless reflection for life itself—just like Narcissus fell in love with his own image and was lost in it, you fall under the world's spell in the same way. You believe in what you see before you, and so are so easily lost because you forget it is merely an image of your own projection.

Divided inside and trapped in a horizontal vision, you can only run after the things you aspire to possess—forgetting they are already yours.

One day, you will realise that there is no place to go, no role to occupy, no power to use in life and no action to undertake for your dream to be realised. Your physical body has to become the most pleasurable place to be, so that the miraculous, the inconceivable, the most wondrous can manifest before your very eyes.

Transformation comes from within.
What you apparently perceive through the body and project into the world outside is only a tiny fragment, represented in time of the timeless universe of your inner being.

You can change something only if you transform yourself!

You have to abandon your destructive way of thinking, of feeling—you have to dream a new dream. You have to learn a new way of dreaming where the power of will commands, where the power of love creates, where the power of certainty wins. By using the inner camera of self-observation, you begin to rise above the level of the ordinary game and a new breathing space, a new aim and sphere of action opens up, revealing how confined you have been for years, how imprisoned and isolated.

Turn your attention towards the Dreamer in you and every limit, calamity, disease and suffering will disappear forever from your world—expand your vision until your whole body, with every organ, muscle, fibre and cells down to the very last atom, is overwhelmed by the light of your dream.

Know that when dreaming is set in motion, all things are possible, as your dreaming contains all the scientific principles for the establishment of the Kingdom of Heaven on earth.

You

When they take away your job or you are full of misery and have no food for your family, or when your son dies in an absurd war, you say that this is not real?

The Dreamer

My answer may appear harsh and lacking compassion, but I want to remind you of a principle that we cannot neglect: 'life is as it is because you are as you are, and it is as much real or unreal as you believe it to be'.

Violence, fear, loneliness, pain, war, birth and death are just concepts generated by your memory and imagination, which are, in their turn, mere shadows and not facts.

You

What are the facts then?

The Dreamer

What you, yourself, are in this precise instant is a fact. You, yourself, free of all fears, are a fact. You, yourself, free of that bundle of lies which constitutes history, tradition, knowledge, religion, culture and experience, are a fact. The timeless you are a fact.

All that which apparently exists in time and which you believe to be external will reduce you to dullness and impotence. Remember! Only what has been 'done' inside is real and can be permanent, the rest is just a short film disintegrating as it is made.

The laws of life reflect an 'inner code' more subtle and invisible. Every time you meet conflicts, disputes or accidents, you must remember that you are projecting that event which is the materialisation of your own internal conflict. If you find yourself in a war, you must have secretly cradled it in your bosom. Yet this is the real crux of the matter, this is what you do not want to admit to and this is what is most difficult to grasp: the acceptance of the fact that what surrounds you is really what you want.

As incomprehensible and paradoxical as it may appear: you have it because you love it!

*You have it because you love it.
You suffer because you enjoy suffering.*

If you enjoy being negative, in whatever forms, you can never observe it and never separate from it. You cannot separate from what you have a secret affection for.

Whatever you identify with, you become.

At the Mercy of Lesser Gods

For thousands of years you've lived at the mercy of lesser Gods—be it through the voice of prophets or that of ideologists, be it through that of scientists, technocrats, statesman or politicians.
Yet nothing has changed. For you, the world remains hopelessly conflictual, violent and mortal.
All attempts to evade through external devices—like music, art, poetry, politics and sciences—have been in vain.

Another Power, then, is needed that's been buried all along in the most hidden recesses of your being, able to defy the law of gravity and challenge the laws of sickness, ageing and death, able to contain and govern the wondrous unpredictability of life: The Will.

Real life is not elsewhere, in some distant ethereal beyond, but down here, in this physical body, which does not die of consumption, but of the absence of light.
It is here, in this body, that everything happens.

It is here, in this body, that we will win the final battle: the idea of the inevitability of death.

You live all your life believing that what is 'out there' has to change before you can change. This is a reactive approach to life which makes you negative, fragmented, fearful and weak.

Stop being reactive!

Anytime you think the problem is 'out there', then that very thought is the problem. In order to accomplish anything remarkable, you must be able to rise above controversies, jealousies, envies and not to react to any petty personal offence or attack.

Being reactive can never change your life. Learn how to change the course of events by being proactive instead, that means to effect change within yourself and not to expect anything coming from 'out there'.

Being proactive is the power to create and move mountains by being still, silent, alert and joyful within.

As a proactive being, you have the power to change your inner states at will, and therefore, the psychological, physical and social conditions of the entire world. If you develop the inner attitude of being proactive, there is no problem or difficulty 'out there' that you cannot control and solve out.

When facing a problem, however small or insurmountable it may appear, simply observe yourself; look within yourself, without judging, without criticising, without identifying; be constantly aware of yourself. This is the only thing that really matters.

In self-awareness, lie all possibilities.

Focus, then, all your attention on now and nothing will ever be impossible to you.

When you learn how to shift your attention from the outer world of probabilities and uncertainties, the world of consequences, then you can open yourself to the limitless inner world of causes, of possibilities and power.

You will see that everything is within you, and that everything is you.

But as long as you are under the illusion that you know yourself, nothing will change for you. You must remember that you are the cause of the world you live in; if you cannot grasp this, you will never be able to explain anything that is happening outside of yourself and you will be tossed about in your life like driftwood on the open sea—your existence will be in chaos, and you will be helpless to do anything about it.

Realise that you have been driven all your life by your negative imagination, and that 'out there', there is no one who'll do you any harm; only you can do that.

Remember yourself and see what appear to be great and menacing giants become but insignificant puppets before you.

It is your complete unawareness of your own deadly schemes that creates all the monsters you find outside of yourself; but anything threatening you in the world has had your consent to exist—it is you who creates the world and you who destroys it.

Even the most heinous criminal, if he could be aware of his own inner self-harmfulness, even if just for an instant, he would become free! It is the awareness of what happens inside you that sets you free. If you become aware of the falsity you carry inside yourself, it will disappear.

All wars, injustice, famine, devastations, crime, catastrophes and every vice of man belongs to you; it is all there inside you to be recognised, put in order and contained.

To put things in order, you need only see them. Your integrity will take care of the rest.

Start by not indulging in any negative thought or resourceful feeling for any length of time. Start by refusing to indulge in any useless, devitalising questions, discussions or circumstances. Start by being aware in any situation of the problems and difficulties without identifying with them. Problems are challenges that you, yourself, create and project to step on and get closer to your inner integrity and perfection.

Remember yourself with all the cells of your body, with all the fibres of your being. Be permanently in a state of full presence and alertness even when there are challenges around you, things falling apart and problems to solve.

You are the source of all, and nothing can happen 'out there' without your inner consent. No one can challenge you 'out there' who is not you. You only and no one else can master your life.

These are 'the rules of the Game'. If you realise this, your inner and outer life will be overwhelmed by victory and success.

Remember! The key to changing reality is self-observation.

We all believe that we observe ourselves, that we are aware of what is going on inside of us, but that is not true. If you could really observe yourself, even if just for a few seconds, you would enter in a state of being that would instantly solve all your problems and open up all possibilities.

When fear, doubt or pain are simply gazed upon without identifying, they tend to dry up and die.

If you could eliminate just an atom of fear from within yourself, you will see appear in front of you a whole new world—a world without violence, a world without war, a world without death.

And yet, to transform your inner being is the most difficult task that you can ever undertake. You will find that to eliminate fear it's impossible, because fear, like death, is a self-created prison and not something that someone else has created or imposed upon you.

The truth is that you are very much attached to your fears; that you are in love with your suffering! If I could eliminate your fears in this very moment, you would suffer much more than before, because you are not ready to be without pain.

For you, to eliminate pain would be more painful than pain itself.

Like billions of people, you go through life completely unaware of the thousands of *small deaths* that occur within you. Like a suicide, every day you are killing yourself—a sort of self-sabotage that for you has become a natural state.

You believe that the purpose of life is to work, make money, to meet people, that you have to be responsible for your organisation, for your family; constantly defending yourself from something 'out there' which is threatening you, attacking you, from an enemy which wants you to fail—and all the while, you are dead inside.

Your failure to recognise and solve yourself within is projecting all sorts of disasters and catastrophes in the outer world. You have created so many difficulties, so many contrasts and so many enemies to the point that you prefer to escape from reality through the only means known to you: physical death.

Like Doctor Frankenstein, you create a monster; you create your own disaster, just to in the end be killed by your own creature! The world you see outside, with all its apparent wars, violence and diseases is the monster that you yourself have created; the very monster that sooner or later you will victimise to be killed!

But life is all right here; you need only capture a glimpse of it and feel it.

Take back control! Be in charge! Today, you begin a new era! You will see that every moment is a beginning that contain and transforms all realities.

So, travel to the ends of the universe within yourself to embrace and understand all that *you are not*, and feel your thoughts slide over you without trying to change anything; just let them pass.

Let it be. Let it be. Let it be…

And in stillness and silence, watch the unveiling of your dream and the creation of a magnificent new world.

You

Science and physics prove to us that in the universe, there are laws, immutable and unquestionable laws, by which, everything is governed. How could I possibly change or affect such forces through my dream?

The Dreamer

There are no laws in the universe but the ones you create.
You are the creator, nobody else. There are no objective rules or overwhelming invisible forces. There is no reality to perceive from outside, but only an apparent, personal world that you yourself are projecting in this very instant.

You
If we have the power to dream the world at will, what shall we dream about?

The Dreamer
Dream for the sake of it. Do not dream to make something happen or to make your dream come true. Dream for the pleasure of dreaming

*Reclaim your identity as creator of the universe.
Free from attraction and repulsion, likes and dislikes, hopes and desires, from attachment and aversion; engaged in various activities, but free from experience; acting various roles, but without believing in them, conditioned neither by pleasure nor by pain.*

*You are the highest of gods in human form,
the fountainhead where everything arises
and where everything also sets.*

*You are, at once, the source and the end of all and
everything.*

Chapter II
Dreaming and Desire

Beliefs, hopes, expectations and desires are all in time, and in time, nothing real can be achieved.

Be right now what you want to be!

There is nothing you have to 'become', no career to chase, no desires to pursue. You only need to enter into the depths of your being and realise you already possess and are everything.

Everyone has desires and goals to achieve; a nicer home, a nicer car, more money, a more creative job, but as a worshipper of time, you're incapable of understanding the difference between desiring and dreaming.

When you hope a situation would get better, wish you were healthier, when you want to be happier or richer, or try to solve a problem, you may not realise that you are 'dreaming' and projecting the very experience of expecting, desiring, hoping, wishing, wanting, needing or trying and that such an experience can only produce exactly the opposite of what you were desiring, wishing or expecting.

For example, if you merely desire to become rich, your inner creative power, acknowledging you as being the Dreamer and creator of your own reality must remove any financial resources and possibilities from your outer life in order that you can be granted the 'experience of desiring' to become rich.

Dream is absence of time; desire is time itself.

Only what is in absence of time can be realised, and that means 'dreaming'. Your reality, whatever it is, is such because you are dreaming it as it is, and your desire to change it cannot come true because desire acts in time.

They let you believe that if you desire something long enough and hard enough, sooner or later, you tend to realise it. They let you believe that after you have paid the price and observed the required laws, the object of your ambition will one day be yours. They taught you to believe that a successful individual has to visualise his success long before it becomes a reality. They let you believe that the constant and dedicated attention to the goal you have set for yourself is the only formula for its achievement.

But remember! Beliefs, hopes, expectations and desires are all in time, and in time, nothing real can be achieved. What you call success, victory, happiness, truth or even financial power can only be produced and released in this very now, by the most real thing that you possess: the Art of Dreaming—the most practical way to hit the mark, win all battles, overcome all limits and achieve the inconceivable.

Be right now what you want to be, and do not desire! If you are whole, in this very instant, you will receive much more than you can ever desire.

Dreaming always comes true, desiring never—because of this, between your dream and your goal, there should be nothing that separates them, no time no desire, nothing should interfere in order for you to succeed.

Imagine yourself experiencing something you don't like. Is it possible to 'want that experience to stop?' Again, you are dreaming and commanding an experience of 'want', of 'desiring' into your own reality while you should be commanding the universe 'what it is that you dream', and not 'what it is that you want'.

Desire is governed by time, fear and doubt, and therefore, can never come true; while the dream creates, loves and takes place in the absence of programs, plans and desires and above all is timeless, that is, creating in this very moment everything that you want. Having comes first, and desire after; meaning that whatever you desire you have to have it before desiring it, so get rid of any sense of desire and approach the object of your desire directly.

We have a distorted interpretation of reality that tells us everything comes from 'outside', and we are helpless before what we have learned to call 'life'. We forget that life is nothing more than a mirroring image of our being, that our every movement emanates a reflection that we call universe, and not recognising ourselves as the source of this projection, we mistakenly think that it has its own independent life, that our reality is made up of a series of events we can't control.

In reality, there are no mistakes in the world's calculation. What you have is what you are, and you cannot have more and neither can you be more, because what you have and what you are is the direct result of what you dream and, by reflection, of what you deserve.

If you could understand that the universe is the perfect projection of your being, you would be commanding the universe 'what it is that you dream,' and not 'what it is that you want, hope, wish or need.'

Think of a significant event in your life, pleasant or not, it doesn't matter, and you will soon realise that the outcome of that event is the final result of your way of dreaming. If there is something you choose to experience in your life, do not 'want it', or 'desire it' but simply, 'be it!'

The one who desires is identified and is mechanically guided by all that which is subject to the forces of gravity and time, thought and imagination. He is a prisoner; he is a victim. The one who dreams instead is guided by an inner pilot who has all things aligned in 'service' to his one aim, his total integrity, and all that he encounters is carefully selected by his power of dreaming to contribute to his evolution and growth.

If your dream is to be more successful, to have a better job, a better life or better health, do not want or desire that. Be that now, down to your very last cell!

This is dreaming—dreaming is such a powerful, creative experience that even few seconds of its timeless action will succeed in creating all that you have desired for years and failed to achieve.

You

What about all the innocent people being killed in the so many wars happening all over the world right now? Certainly, they desire for such horrors to stop?

The Dreamer

People killing each other in Afghanistan, in Iraq, in Palestine and in many other countries are certainly 'desiring to come out of that hell' but the very experience of 'coming out of that hell' is not what they are going to experience, but rather 'the state of desiring' itself, which cannot change anything and it is, paradoxically, the very cause of the condition they are living in.

If you want a negative event or experience to disappear from your world, you have 'to stop wanting that experience to disappear'.

Your inner power, acknowledging you as being the creator of your own reality doesn't allow that experience to disappear in order that you can be granted 'the very experience of wanting or desiring'.

You

And the children dying of starvation in Africa?

The Dreamer

I will answer you, although what I am going to say will appear cynical and merciless, and more than anything, lacking of compassion and solidarity.

Stop your false attitude of worrying about the others, which is the very cause of all the hypocrisy and crime in the world. Stop being in 'need' of helping people and no one will ever be asking for help, and, difficult to understand, hunger and starvation will disappear from the Earth.

It's 'you, yourself, in need' which is creating and projecting a world in need, a world of suffering and pain, a world without resources, starving and dying.

'Being in need' is a mere self-sabotage, another way of harming or killing yourself inside, so therefore the world that you produce cannot be other than the reflection of your nightmare of anger, guilt, misery and death.

A creator never tries to do or create anything specifically. A creator never tries to change his own creation. A creator simply creates. A lover simply loves. A Dreamer simply dreams.

You

But what about philanthropy? What about the thousands of charitable foundations and organisations that have made it their life's work to help the ones in need?

The Dreamer

There are organisations that only exist to perpetuate themselves. They specialise in obtaining funds and gathering resources which they then misspend and squander, barely managing to support themselves. If you lift the smoke-screen surrounding philanthropy in its every form, you might discover that behind the suffragists and the Salvation Armies, behind medical and pharmaceutical aid, behind the distribution of food and shelter, behind the battles for the recognition of human rights, behind the apparent lavishness for the rescue of migrates and political refugees, hides the most atrocious organised crime and the worst acts against mankind.

Don't waste your time in feeling pity or compassion for someone. No one can do anything for anybody. The harder their condition, the greater the opportunity. It is up to them to seize the chance.

Everything happens for a reason and a purpose.

Remember! Man dies because he lies. He who has not defeated the lie within himself, he who is unaware of the self-sabotage that constantly goes on within him, cannot do anything for anyone.

Most of people spend all their lives chasing the idea of becoming experts in some specific field of human knowledge, believing that one day, the object of their studies, research and exploration can pay them back with fame, money and glory. Others believe that all the resources, time and efforts they invest upon the noble task of improving the conditions of humanity will one day be affirmed and recognised.

But behind all this, a meticulous trap is well prepared. Behind the very aim of serving and loving humanity, secretly buried into the innermost recesses of their being, the very cause of all failures governs—that is, the lie of loving the world more than themselves—a state of presumption and vain imagination that they will save the world, and in the end, the expectation for an outer recognition or reward that, due to this inner condition, will never come.

Remember! If you first love yourself inside, the world will be safe for good, and all wealth, goodness and beauty will naturally follow. But every man on earth is trapped in a virtual reality, in a nightmare he can't get out of until he realises he himself is the Dreamer.

A show is always a show, even if it depicts something horrible. Forgetting it and trying to help it or change it through external means is to lose oneself in identification and death. It means to cease to be the cause and become the effect.

If you're aware of being the creator of the reality you encounter, you can't be a victim.

Whatever happens in life is always for your good. And if something apparently goes against your expectations or doesn't fulfil your desires, that simply means that you don't understand how your dream is taking care of you. When you wish to change something in your life and are in a 'state of desire', you find your situation either continuing unchanged, or worsening because you should be commanding into the universe 'what it is that you dream' and not 'what it is that you hope, wish, or expect'. Asking for any help weakens your intuitive, creative power of doing.

Stop being in need and you will not believe how easy it is to gain all the resources you apparently need. Stop asking for help! Stop desiring! Stop depending! One of the most effective ways to making your dream come true is to feel right now the very experience of its realisation. Being in contact with your inner being makes you feel in this very instant a deep sense of certainty, clarity and safety, which is the very cause for every victory and success in life.

You are the very creator of the world you are living in, and as such, you can only create and never be created or helped by anyone or anything coming from outside. And more than anything, free yourself from the need of helping the world.

There is no one who needs or asking for help. You all are self-hypnotised from the fact that there is someone who suffers 'out there'. But the 'out there' is inside you. Therefore, stop suffering and the world will cease to suffer. Stop being in need.

Stop dying inside, and the entire world, every human being will live forever in justice, harmony and beauty.

Dream and reality are one and the same thing.

The dream is always fulfilled because between dream and reality, there is no causal relationship. They are not divided by Time. So, do not indulge or identify with your worries, fears or desires. Let them come and go. Be free. Freedom means essentially free from identifying yourself with desire and fear. Even the desire of knowing the truth one day will have to be abandoned to make further progress possible.

Remember! Never desire, never ask, never beg—not even for heaven! A beggar can never make it. Prayer and meditation, even for the sake of grace, truth or God, can only create more distance between you and what you are asking for.

Be…and become. Simply be…and you'll become whatever you want to.

Forget the hypnotic, mortal description of the world with its unreasonable logic and aimless planning. Close your eyes and open yourself up to intuition. The world is still waiting for you to be created.

For me, it's impossible to accept the idea that whatever happens in life is always for my good and that only good news exists. What about if a young person very dear to you dies, do you think you receive such news and react to it as the arrival of good news?

The Dreamer

You have to understand that whatever happens outside yourself has to have your inner approval and consent to manifest. This means that anything happening in your own life is the faithful reflection of your will power in action.

You have it because you love it, this is the law.

If you unconsciously love blaming, complaining, self-justifying, accusing or indulging in self-pity, anger and suffering, that very dear person dies to make you realise your hidden, mortal vision of life as the very cause of all your dreary, gloomy experiences.

It may be very hard for you to accept, but remember! Anything that allows you to understand and realise the truth about yourself, even if unbearable, is always good news.

You

My only desire has always been to help people and give to the world. Is also this desire something I have to get rid of?

The Dreamer

You can give to the world only what you truly give to yourself.
Self-giving is the sole, real giving.
A man of integrity takes from within and knows that before expressing any energy in the outer world he must learn how to stop inner leakage.
Leakage means forgetfulness.
You spend all your energy in the wrong way—on identification and negative emotions, complaining and accusation, on lying and idle talks. These are open taps from which your energy runs out. Stop this leakage and you will accumulate an enormous amount of energy.
Remember! You are the very root of the world. You are the inexhaustible source that nurtures all and everything.
You are the Supreme Vision and the infinite reality. That means that you are the giver and the receiver at the same time.

You

What about egoistic, greedy people who can only take from the world.

The Dreamer

Nobody can take anything from the world because the world has nothing to give.

You are the sole Dreamer, producer and the only distributor, and the world is only a shadow, a pale reflection of what you really are. Not even the most clever thief can ever steal anything from you without your 'consent'.

Something can be taken away from you, including your life, only if you first 'give it up'.

Dream if You Want to Change

*The only way you can change the reality you are living in is to dream a new world,
to project a new vision.
Your life is such because you don't know how to bring any change in your own
dream, even if you're living hell.*

*Remember! It is impossible to find yourself in a war if you don't produce death
within yourself, if you don't dream of it.
War, poverty, failure, disease, death or any other disaster are not objective
realities. They are not outside you.
They become real only if you dream of them.*

*To be a politician, you have to produce conflicts, within and without, although you
pretend to fight for peace.
To be a journalist, you have to produce scandals,
and first of all, within yourself,
That's why your life is a catastrophe.
To be a doctor, you have to materialise illnesses and viruses, the same ones that
one day will kill you.*

Don't try to change or modify anything external, you will fail. Go within without swerving, without deviating, without ever looking outward and... Be! Just be! And the entire world will be lifted up into the perfect state.

We are constantly in a state of expectation; we expect certainty from the others: protection, gratification, happiness, but all that arrives from outside can only last for a moment. So, don't worry about the world, worry about yourself. It could seem like an egotistic approach, but real doing is only for oneself, inside. You would like to do for the others, but there is nothing you can do for anyone if you don't become the shadow of your own creation.

Life can be transformed only by changing your dream, that is, by turning something lower into something higher, something coarser into something finer. Your position and role in life are determined by the quality of your own being, the breadth of your vision and the power of your own will.

It's time then to unbury the will! Will exists only in the now. You can't exercise it on the world; the world and the others are time and the will can only act in the absence of time. The world can only follow. What seems to come from the world is only an effect projected in time by the will. The will is the 'non doing', which is the real 'doing'.

'Mavens non motum'. In the absence of time, through the will, you can create in yourself all that you want: happiness, wealth, joy and beauty. But while we program and plan, we project an imaginary future that makes us defer from this very instant, the only time in which real action can occur. You believe that the world has powers and abilities to decide, that it can recognise your merits and qualities, and so you wait for a feeling of gratification, which either never arrives or lasts only but a moment because it is false.

The world follows your steps, obeys your inner states, but if these aren't governed by the will, they are like crazy monkeys jumping from one branch to another. When you realise that all is decided and depends on you, you will not waste any more time in worrying about the others but only about your change.

The terrible condition of man is that of being the author of the world in which he lives, and at the same time the victim of his own creation. It is the identification with the world which puts you in a state of expectation and dependence. In reality, this Work is just about learning how to be in the world without identifying with it, keeping an arrow of attention pointed always towards yourself and another one towards the world outside; this is called 'double attention'.

You have to realise that the only way to intervene in the game of the world is an inner action, which is the transformation of yourself.

Then, do not complain if things go wrong, but enter into yourself and get rid of all the unnecessary sufferings, destructive thoughts, self-imposed narrowness. Enter into yourself and stay 'there', fearlessly facing your sorrow and confusion. Stay 'there' and do not blame anybody for your misery and unhappiness.

Stay 'there' and don't move until you 'win'.

Whatever you want to achieve in your life, always remember:
'Do not desire, deserve'.

You

How can it be that desire never comes true? I first loved, desired something and then I really possessed it.

The Dreamer

You are right when you say, 'First, I loved'. To possess something, you have to be responsible for it, you have to love, you have to be in a state of absence of death, and then only, you can receive something or someone you believe to have desired.

This is difficult to understand. The object, the event, the person that you apparently desire, or even the financial position you occupy in the society is only the shape, an outer form of something invisible: your inner state of responsibility and love.

Health is wealth; the more you love yourself inside, the richer, in all senses, is your life.

You
You say that we should stop desiring, but if desires disappear then what remains?

The Dreamer
All that which can never change, the truth, the intelligence, the beauty of this world, remains. The infinite, almighty, immeasurable 'you', remains.

You

What about the desire to win? To be the best? Surely, this inner drive is the most important factor in every successful individual.

The Dreamer

Rather than feed the desire to win, you have to unravel and eliminate your hidden willingness to lose.

How you do it? By becoming aware of this diabolic self-sabotage and dreary self-deception. Victory is an innate, permanent state of being, and as such, can materialise in the external world only when you are aware of it, that is, when you will know how to win yourself inside by overcoming and going beyond, once and for all, your self-imposed condition of suffering and destructiveness.

You

I understand that my question may appear vain and materialistic, but my dream is to become rich. How can I achieve this?

The Dreamer

This is impossible to achieve because you cannot become what you already are.

What you have to do is to get free of all that which impedes your inner power to manifest.
Stop indulging in what you are not: unhappy, sad, poor, at war with yourself, and in an instant, you will possess everything you think you do not have; freedom, ease, success, financial power and love!
Quality is power. Quality creates quantity and not vice versa. The level of your inner freedom determines your financial fortune. If you want to be rich, you have to hold all your attention where the only freedom in the universe comes from: your own inner being.

There is no authority higher than you. No authority can give you happiness, joy, comfort or wealth. You are the highest authority that gives, loves, dares and dreams from the inside.

The integrity of your being makes you inevitably rich.

You

I consider myself very fortunate. I have everything a man can desire, and yet I feel very anxious. I am always afraid that everything I possess can be lost in a fraction of a second.

The Dreamer

Since there is nothing existing but yourself, what are you afraid of? You should focus only on the totality of yourself as your true world. Real life is only inside and nobody can take anything away from you without your consent.

You

But we are all worried about tomorrow, about the future, the precariousness of the future. How can we deal with this uncertainty?

The Dreamer

First of all, ask yourself what 'time' is all about, what is its very meaning. Time is a trap, a painful, mortal, self-created prison. Time is a crime generated by your own way of thinking. So, thought is time, and time breeds fear, and fear creates all that which you are afraid of. In the powerful state of inner awareness, time will disappear and with it, all the absurdities, illusions and contradictions of this world.

You

Without fear and desire, what motive is there in life for action?

The Dreamer

Do not be afraid of getting rid of fear and desire. When their projected image vanishes, you should not feel at a loss before a blank screen, but dive deeper within to embrace the new heaven and new earth you have only just discovered.

When fear and desire are gone, the real power of doing is revealed, and you will live a life much more intense and interesting than you can ever imagine.

Victim of the Visible

Your age long belief in the description of the world and in the others as an entity outside yourself is very strong, misleading and deceitful, and now you feel you haven't got a clue as to how to arrive at an inner integrity.

For you to attain unity seems so difficult because it is impossible to become what you already are.

Unity of being is simply the acknowledgement of yourself as a self-making god, but you have forgotten your divine nature and have become a 'victim of the visible'.

When you go into the world, the tangible overwhelms you.

You are so easily taken in and trapped by the symbols and shadows of power, you encounter outside—conditioned by the desire for money, fame or success.

Without the principles of the work, you go into the world and find yourself in front of something which appears to be immense, obscure and conflictual. You fumble in the darkness of your ignorance like a blind man without a cane—problems seem insurmountable, goals unachievable.

You desperately try to grasp the object of your desire through external means, forgetting that all comes from within and that vision and reality are one and the same!

Remember yourself! Through self-awareness, you will realise one day that you're not that tiny little bundle of desires and fears, of misery and pain, that fleeting flash of consciousness lost in an ocean of darkness, but the everlasting, omnipotent being, supremely happy, creator, sustainer and transformer of all there is, the source of all life, the Dreamer and the dreamed, the beingness of all beings.

'You man, understand yourself and you will understand the gods and universe'.
Inscription on the shrine of the *Oracle of Delphi*,
1400 BC—Ancient Greece

Being in contact with your inner being makes you feel in this very instant a deep sense of certainty, clarity and safety, which is the very cause for every victory and success in life.

Many turn towards the practices of meditation, and yoga in an attempt to come in touch with their inner selves, and to overcome the many difficulties in their lives.

But meditation is not the answer, and through meditation, you will never be able to understand what I am telling you. Meditation is another way to indulge and deceive yourself; it is just another way for sleeping.

Meditation, like yoga, shamanism, transhumanism and all self-improvement disciplines and techniques, have become industries, just another merchandise to sell and intoxicate the masses. This work is about abandoning all masters, teachers and all the 'spiritual junk' which you chose to keep on lying to yourself.

You have gone from worldly desires to celestial ones, but they are desires nonetheless.

To desire God or love is not different from desiring money and power; it is just the same thing. You are always in a state of desiring nonetheless. This is not dreaming. It is not the dream. And this is why you will never obtain the object of your desire—but only the very experience of your desiring.

You will believe to enter into another dimension through meditation, prayer or contemplation, but nothing will change; you will always remain in the same mess.

Instead of meditating, which is just an excuse to indulge in an endless expectation, or begging for some celestial or divine award; pierce instead the age-old layers of descriptions and lies—deeper and deeper until you reach a state of inner stillness and silence.

Only then, in a state of fearlessness and deathlessness, you will be able to experience 'real doing': the only power to change the reality you are living in.

Freedom from sorrow has to be the only aim, so cut down all other cravings, even the one for truth or for God and focus all your attention on your inner being. If you can free yourself from your inner agony, you will find yourself in an entirely different world.

The moment you observe the battle of opposites that goes on within yourself, the fear dies. It dies as a seed when it breaks its skin to give way to a brand new life.

*Do not indulge in false ideas, useless sensations or fantasies.
Spirituality is for those who do not want to recognise and come out of their own inner violence.
'People die because they bargain their own will for doctrine'.*

You

Throughout my life, I have prayed and meditated, I have experimented with all kinds of disciplines and techniques, all in an attempt to win pain and unhappiness. But I have found my efforts to be unrewarding; the world around me seems more and more threatening, and now I'm left with nothing but disappointment and loneliness.

The Dreamer

Don't try to avoid unhappiness when it comes.
You need to be willing and strongly determined to throw yourself into the abyss of sorrow, into mouth of evil. Without blaming the others, turn towards yourself and touch this physical pain that you wrongly believe to be caused from something external.
Touch it, and you will realise that that pain comes only from within, that it has always been there—there where you have never dared to adventure; where the nausea, the sorrow and defeat reside.
You may have lived a tremendous life, travelled all over the world, acquired a great deal of knowledge, searched and practiced every kind of ideology, religion or discipline, but all that has nothing to do with the immeasurable now, which is the sole, real freedom.

Remember! You are unique and the revelation of this uniqueness is the task and the purpose of our work.

You

So what is the purpose of religion? Why, in an age of such technological advancements, so many people seem to still follow its practices and be under its influence?

The Dreamer

The hidden purpose of every religion, philosophy, ideology, science or technology has always been to show 'how to do, how to create, how to change the world around at will'—but such purpose is now all but lost and distorted in empty and meaningless rituals and external activities.

On the contrary, the power of doing is not an external technique that you can acquire, but your inner integrity in action. There are no rituals or technique to follow in order to increase your power of doing, but simply to struggle against your love of being negative—to give up your secret love for suffering. To increase your power of doing, you have to make room to something you have neglected and forgotten for so many years—your inner will.

Your inner will is the very cause of all success, of all victory and of all that which takes form in the world of events and has to be renewed every day through self-observation, through self-love and understanding.

You
Then are austerities and disciplines of any use?

The Dreamer
To meet gratefully whatever life brings is all the austerity you need.

Don't invent self-inflicted tortures through useless disciplines. Accept what comes as it comes. One day, you will realise that everything in the world is part of your conscious creativity, and that you don't need any discipline to become what you already are: the cause of all causes.

You

What about those who preach the principles of the Dreamer? Do you think that the Dreamer ideas and studies could ever become a religion?

The Dreamer

Religion cannot be confused with the non-teaching of the Dreamer. His sole purpose is to raise the intelligence and aliveness of those around him albeit, on more than one occasion, against their very will and beyond their understanding.

The popularity of the Dreamer will give rise to false teachers. They can speak of integrity, inner impeccability and freedom, power of doing and love, but they themselves are slaves in their heart of their own vanity, presumption and misunderstanding.

They are the ones who speak in the name of the Dreamer, his principles and ideas, only for speculation and money. They are the ones who commit all kinds of crimes and errors in the name of loyalty and love. They are the ones who cause oppression and persecution in the name of freedom.

Their dishonesty, their deception will be unveiled and exposed in all its hypocrisy when they will try to teach or preach the principles of the Dreamer.

Remember, the School for Gods cannot be taught, but only lived and experienced close to the Dreamer.

The Laws of the Deuteronomy

'You shall not covet your neighbour's house. You shall not covet your neighbour's wife, or his manservant or maidservant, his ox or donkey or anything that belongs to your neighbour'.

Exodus 20:17 (NIV)

The commandment to not covet, closely examined, reveals itself as a great law of economy. The wisdom of Israel, though with different formulas due to the changes of the social and cultural contexts, inserts in the decalogue, attributing it to Yahweh, which means 'I am', the most simple yet fundamental of principles: do not desire!

Unlike the meaning that we give nowadays to the term 'desire', the classical conception indicated it as something negative and harmful to man with reference to its etymology:

Desiderium = de / sidera, drifting apart from the stars.

Those ancient laws reveal the deceit in which we fall, the instinct for power and possession, and the belief that something outside ourselves can complete or enrich us. When a man desires, there is a shift of the focal point: not projected towards its own evolution, but aiming to achieve the wishes of others and enslaved by the objects desired.

But all that you are creating within yourself cannot belong to others, you're not desiring it but *dreaming it.*

Dreams and reality is one and the same thing.

The goal is neither fair nor near, and there is no distance to cross nor time to count.

In eternity, all is here and now.

The obstacles that you find outside are the limits you carry inside. Invest totally on the most real thing that you have: the dream.

Recognise yourself as the sole creator of your reality, and your dreams will instantly come true. Invest everything you have and everything that you do not have in something you buried and forgot: your will.

To be a King means to be in absence of time; that is to be fearless, guiltless, desire-less, whole.

*To be a king, you have to love and love like dreams
cannot be in time.
Love cannot be planned, organised or measured.
Real love can only happen now.*

*Remember! You cannot dream a
kingdom, you can only desire a
kingdom, that's why it can never happen.*

Be a king and the kingdom will come!

If you are whole, in this precise instant, you will receive much more than you might ever desire.

Chapter III
The Art of Acting

Act your role in life as a great actor does on the stage, always.

Believe without believing!

Free from identification and capable of acting in life as an impeccable actor, a man finds solutions, decides things and overcomes impossible issues, wins battles and conflicts, climbs mountains and crosses oceans through his own inner states, that is, within himself, in solitude, in silence, in stillness.

Any organisation, business or teamwork he creates is just the outer expression of his inner responsibility, and it is as faithful and intelligent as his own incorruptible commitment to the dream.

He never asks for anything because he knows that no help can come from outside. He knows that within himself, he's got all the capacity and the strength to attract all the resources he needs.

He knows that the only tool necessary for his victory and success in the world of events is his own inner integrity.

'Acting' is the 'Art of Dreaming' in action.

Before you realise that the others are the exact reflection of your own being, the perfect expression of your inner creativity, you have to learn and practice the 'art of acting'.

'Acting' requires you to consciously put yourself in the 'shoes' of others and see yourself in them and them in yourself. You have to listen to them internally and find the same thing in yourself. When you consciously 'act', you do not blame or criticise, but accept the others as an expression of your creativity, the materialisation of your inner states and attitudes. You cannot change or improve the others, in the same way in which you cannot change the reflection in the mirror, without recognising yourself as its very source.

You have to dream within and 'act' without.

Dreaming and acting is one and the same thing. A man of integrity, a Dreamer, acts his role intentionally and impeccably, playing his part in the world perfectly as his dream commands.

Acting intentionally is more real than the reality they taught you to believe. The belief of an ordinary man is total identification. It doesn't matter if you identify with an object or with God. Identification is always death, and only a man free from identification can stay alive in a world that demands his total involvement.

There is nothing wrong with playing and nothing wrong with the role you act. The problem arises only when you forget to act and identify with the role itself. You have to just act your part without believing.

It's the not believing that makes things happen! It's the *believing without believing*! This is the only way to go through life—to conquer yourself. The ability to believe without believing is the power to contain yourself and not be taken in by either circumstances or events. As soon as you lose the awareness that everything is a projection of yourself, you are at the mercy of your pain—of your unconscious suffering.

Acting is freedom. Acting is truth. Acting is the only way you can bring to others what they couldn't even dream of. It is your ability to act which determines, in the theatre of life, whether you will be rich or poor, a winner or a loser.

You can survive only if you act impeccably the role the circumstances require. When you stop acting, you are dead.

You have the duty to remember to be the scriptwriter, director and producer of this incredible picture—show you call reality and that everyone is playing the part that you assigned to them. Even you, the creator, are called to act!

A man who has learned to act knows that everyone he meets is a projection of his dream. They are all parts of a representation: a huge movie set, with thousands of background actors who play their role without being aware of it, believing it real, all committed to convince you that you are one of them too.

But when you forget yourself and identify with the game, you fall prey to the same illusion, you lose your role as creator and protagonist of the show, and become a background actor as all the others, a frame of the same movie, a shadow...

Acting intentionally your role makes you more real than the reality in which you are called to act.

Acting consciously, is the practical way to overcome all difficulties—playing your role intentionally is the power of the will in action.

A man of integrity is able to recite perfectly in any circumstance the required role without identifying with the play of life. He knows that the moment he falls in the trap of believing that the world is a separate reality, he will lose his status as a creator and become a victim of his own forgetfulness.

Through the art of acting, you will learn how to wear the right mask in any circumstances, to perform impeccably any social and economic status—to act all roles perfectly, especially the ones most hated, in order for you to be free from them.

Before he can break out of the prison of his roles, a man must feel disappointed with the sterile repetitiveness of the events and circumstances of his own life.

Remember, the freedom from a role and the ability to transcend it only comes when you have learned to act it perfectly. When you perform a role impeccably, and act it perfectly, it not only frees you, but also the world of its own misery and violence.

You

Isn't acting the same as lying?

The Dreamer

Many of you have wrongly understood the meaning of the 'art of acting' and confused it with the unconscious, mechanical habit of lying. Lying means self-deceiving. Lying means dying. When you lie to others, you are creating and projecting a world of troubles, failure and injustice. When you lie to the Dreamer, you have killed in yourself the only possibility for self-transformation and growth and will be inevitably catapulted into the deadly ghetto of despair and misery. Be very careful! Every attempt from your part to use the 'art of acting' as a way of living without the proper, conscious understanding of it, will transform your life into the inescapable prison of hypocrisy and death.

Observe yourself and watch what is false in you. Lying damages all possibilities to work on yourself. Lying prevents any development of your inner being and consequently any achievement and success in your outer life. Lying kills your dream, the most real thing in you. As you are, you cannot stop lying unless you get to know yourself by long, sincere accurate work of self-observation.

You
Does not acting in life take away spontaneity?

The Dreamer
Consciously acting gives you a greater spontaneity and power.

You

How can I act the love for my child, or the grief for my parents passing? Would this not result in me being insincere?

The Dreamer

Sincerity means to consciously act like a good actor, how to be sincere.

To be sincere, you must touch that most real part of yourself and simultaneously reflect it in the world of events—this is acting. If you stop acting, you get lost in the multitude of useless roles and false truths. If you stop acting, you die!

Acting impeccably what you are called to act in any circumstances makes you free. Strategically wearing the right mask to satisfy the expectations of the world around is the only way to survive in a world that you yourself have created and projected. Remember! A role, any role in life is a prison. For many years, your false sincerity has brought you to act the role of a machine that with other machines is slave of an unknown, invisible design and obeys the command of an infernal project. You have been acting all your life, but unconsciously believing that this was real life. Now, you are called to act the same role, the same life, but this time without believing in it, and consciously knowing that life is an incredible game, a beautiful show that you have staged through 'The Art of Dreaming'.

You

Then should we never be ourselves? Should we be constantly playing a role?

The Dreamer

You have to understand that when you say: 'should we be ourselves or act', you are still deceiving yourself. You are lying. How can you be yourself if you do not know who you are? If you don't know what it means to 'be yourself'?

What I am telling you is to instead observe what you are not! Discover and understand what you are not, because your life is just what you are not, not what you are.

You are always acting, whether you know it or not. The Art of Acting is simply playing a role by conscious choice.

Man lives all his life in a state of identification, of forgetfulness, constantly distracted, disorganised and uncertain; that is why life manifests itself in all its theatrical madness. But what is outside, what you call reality is harmless, inexistent. It is only our identification that makes the unreal real. The apparent hostility, unfairness, violence and injustice in the world are all valuable elements to understand and practice the Art of Acting, and how to remain intact and whole inside at all times.

The moment you observe the struggle of opposites within, your fear dies. It dies just as a seed dies and gives way to a new life. Observing your inner war without identifying with it awakens you to a higher dimension, eliminating all forms of conflict and injustice in the world of events.

When you remember yourself, you feel certain, always at rest and entirely safe. This is the only moment you are real—the only moment you can join a leading role in life.

But be careful not to lie! Only if you learn to recite your part perfectly, you can survive and escape the surveillance of careful guards—'The Snipers of the Invisible'—that you yourself have put in place to prevent you from getting into roles of a higher order. When you act impeccably, you will know the role-play and you will know how to transcend them.

The art of acting is the most important technique for those who are firmly committed to return to their lost integrity and freedom.

In the ancient, sacred scriptures of the Vedas, the Art of Acting is called *Karma-Yoga,* to do all things, all kind of work or activity and occupying any role in life without identifying with it, be it success or failure.

Remember! In the game of life, you will be called to play all kinds of roles, from a beggar to a tycoon, and you must learn to recite it perfectly without any reserves. The problem arises only when you forget to act and identify with the role itself. Whatever you identify with has power over you. Identification means slavery. Be flexible in life, and remember your aim: to master the art of acting. This is the key to survival; when you act a role consciously, and perform it perfectly, it not only frees you, but also the entire world of its own misery and violence.

Identification means fusing with something so totally as to dissolve into it and completely cease to exist.

A man can identify himself with an idea, with an unpleasant emotion or event or person, thus ceasing to exist as an individual, as a whole and becoming part of something else.

Remember! You become that which you identify with. If you find yourself in a state of limitation, poverty or failure, you are unconsciously and secretly worshipping them.

When feelings of helplessness and despondency arise, do not despair; stay still. Observe them without identifying, breathe deeply, persevere in your self-transformation and you shall pierce eternity.

You

How can I discover who I am and who I want to be if, as you say, I have to be always acting a role in life?

The Dreamer

You can only observe what you are not.

Look inside yourself; you can only look at what you are not, what you 'are' you can only 'be'! In that moment, there is no space, no time, no role, nothing to do and nowhere to go. That is the perception of the 'seed' of what you are.

For a fraction of a second, you are nobody and yet you possess all that which surrounds you. It has nothing to do with thoughts, feelings or inner dialogues; in a fraction of a second, you are suspended in a higher emotional state. It is another plane of existence where thoughts and feelings do not come into play.

It is a matter of being, that's all.

You

What is the truth? Who is imagining whom? Are you imagining me or am I imagining you?

The Dreamer

The truth cannot be described, it must be experienced. For now, focus all your attention on the fact that you are the 'One without alterity'.

Acting Is Surrender

*Acting gives you the opportunity to pass unobserved through the Gateway of the Impossible, and to escape
the destiny of a slave.*

In acting, you can be anyone or anything from a king to a peasant, yet always the king inside.
Acting is the act of a warrior. Conscious acting is more real than the reality itself you have been taught to believe.

For a warrior, there is nothing more glorious than a battle which arrives unprovoked and unexpected.
A warrior faces the battle of life remaining untouched in happiness and pain, gain and loss, in victory and defeat.

The believing of an ordinary man is identification—whilst believing without believing requires the qualities of an impeccable actor.

Only a free man can remain free in a world that 'requires' his identification.

Be free inside!

Recite your role in life like a great actor on stage—always.
This is believing without believing, this is the technology of the Dreamer.

The Unity That Pulses

You create heaven and earth, within and without, good and evil; the game of life is expressed in the world of duality through opposites.

You must be able to live in the world of conflicts with the knowledge that behind all the opposites, there is a harmony, a unity that pulses.

> '*A young man asked Buddha if he could become his disciple.*
>
> *"Have you ever stolen?" asked Buddha.*
> *"No, never!" replied the young man.*
>
> *"Then go and steal," said Buddha, "and then come back to me."*'

Holiness contains crime. You must know all the roles and all the levels to reach unity. If that role is missing in self-knowledge, it must, in time and in space, be balanced.

In time and space, we are not able to see that the opposites are the same thing. First one, then the other shows itself and we are not able to see the unity that pulses within ourselves.

Buddha's 'go and steal', is the unity that pulses behind apparent opposites.

The Chant of Humanity

Look through a day; take it as the epitome of your life. Notice the words you say, the feelings and thoughts you express, the physical sensations you experience—classify them, single out the most frequent ones, those that you live and express more often... You will realise that as a whole, you are quite a monotonous being.

If you pay a bit of attention, you will in fact realise there is nothing new in your sensations, that everything in your day is a constant repetition, and that like a machine you are programmed to feel certain sensations, to experience certain emotions, to have certain thoughts, to pronounce certain words... You are like a musical instrument that vibrates at a given pace, and can emit only that sound—and as such, you are occupying only a very narrow band in the infinite of possible keys, vibrations and sounds.

You will realise that every day, you sing the same song and that the external world, what you call reality, does nothing but obey to that rhythm, that sound, that vibration.

> *A man's reality, his ability to do and therefore to have, his degree of happiness as well as his financial destiny, is nothing more but the perfect representation of his 'rate of vibration'.*

The world can only be as narrow or as large as the wideness or narrowness of your song; so ask yourself: "What song am I singing?" It is the same as questioning yourself about your destiny.

When you will be able to listen to it, when you will take more care of the notes you utter, you will be able to notice its mono-tony; then also your will and your ability to widen this pentagram will rise. Like a piano, that with respect to other instruments, has such a vastness of octaves to use two pentagrams, so there are men who have a much wider expressive range than others do; men who play a music that spreads on three, four, five pentagrams... Because their dream is too wide to be contained in the narrow band that suffices the rest of mankind.

Two men make business because of this fusion of rhythms; this consistency of sounds... This harmony. Likewise, a firm takes over another firm for the wideness of its music; a civilisation conquers another civilisation and absorbs it for the vastness of its chant, the wideness of octaves, the quality of its sounds, the richness, the power of its music.

One day, your being will be so wide that you will be able to listen to not only yours, but also to the song of others... The sounds that others utter... The profoundness and the height of their octaves... Of their notes' colour, timbre, rhythm. When you will be ready to stand up to the responsibility of this truth, you will realise that humanity sings a song of misfortune, pain, doubt, fear; that it thinks and feels negatively.

You will see that only apparently man wishes himself wealth, prosperity, health, but that if he could observe and know himself inwardly, he would hear a continuous recitation of a chant of negativity, a prayer of doom made by preoccupations, sick images and the unconscious desire for terrible events to occur, both probable and improbable.

Watch the difficulty of changing even a single word of your daily lexicon: an accent, an interlayer. Watch the inability to change an attitude, a reaction, stop a routine and get out of a mechanical repetition of gestures and sounds. Just imagine what it might mean to transform a thought, change an emotion. Look at yourself unable to pick up a new idea, to accept it and dive into the invisible, to dream something original, something seemingly impossible, to play a single note that comes out of the state in which you are forced to live.

You will realise that it is easier to move a mountain. You'll find that the process of ageing and hardening began some time ago and that soon, you will not be able to fight it anymore.

Rich men and poor men, tycoons and employees, gods and common men: each one with its own song, each one in their own prison, sealed in a bubble, crucified in their role, in their habits. Most of humanity is obedient to a mechanical program established by birth, repeated in childhood; performs a hypnotic music learned from bad musicians, monotonous teachers, prophets of dooms, by parents who cannot do more than pass on the song that they learned.

There are great musicians, titans ranging between staves of existence, they create and capture their music from within. Once that this is understood, a man can have no other aim in his life than escaping from this narrow range in which all humanity is imprisoned from the monotony and poverty of its own music.

There is no bigger project, no war is more sacred than the one fought against your own limits and for raising your chant.

Music coming from within is the power of doing.

If you want to change your reality, you have to change your music.

You have to devote yourself to widening your Dream; because it is your dream that creates reality, and only your dream can rescue you out of this tight spot of being, out of your chant's monotony, that becomes pain in your body, fear in your feelings and doubt in your mind.

If you study yourself, if you observe yourself, day by day you will be able to broaden your dream, moving, creating and modifying its elements. Every day, you will realise more and more that the dream is more real than your illusionary life.

Through dreaming, you will create relationships, solve problems, enter inaccessible worlds. You will learn how to dive into the invisible. Reality will follow, and will take your dream's shape and dimension.

Knowing yourself is discovering that man is alone in the universe, sole responsible for anything happening to him. So have the courage to dream. Have the courage to be an individual and conquer all that is possible to conquer…within.

Know the song you sing, know thyself as the creator of anything you see, you feel, you desire… Know thyself as the only one existing…

This Earth is a beautiful thought.
So transform this Earth in a paradise… It is all up to you.

You

I have dedicated my entire life to music, and I've done my job. I played the clarinet with the greatest jazz musicians in the world, compared to many I feel lucky having found something in music that made me famous and gave me everything I wanted; but despite this, today I feel the saddest man in the world.

The Dreamer

All your life, you have believed in the role that you have been called to play and now at your age, you're realising that the mask belonged to your false personality and not to you.

Now you are here to learn to play the roles consciously. The role is always a lie if it is not acted intentionally—and your identification with the role imprisons you and makes you unhappy. In order to be a musician, you have to be a liar; you have to lie to yourself.

Now I'll talk to you about the real 'music'. Beyond the music, there is silence. Besides the action, there is the action 'without action', the doing 'without doing'. When you have discovered the real music, the silence within yourself, you will no longer be able to play. You came here to listen to these words. If you don't hang the clarinet on the wall, it will be the clarinet that hangs you.

If you lie, you die. You can die only if you lie. If you stop lying, you will live forever.

Musicians and artists are often incomplete people, they are sad and call their sorrow—art.

Never forget! The highest art is to build your own integrity.

*You can only act if you remember the
principles of the school.*

*Acting means taking others into consideration and doing not only what is
pleasant to you, but what is right and pleasant to them.*

*Acting impeccably means knowing which role you are called to play in all
circumstances to satisfy the expectations of others.*

Believing Without Believing

*There is no fault, no sin, no karma or punishment.
There is no life beyond and no universal judgment, no heaven and no hell. There is only this instant, sacred, infinite and omnipotent.
Use it well! You will never have another chance.*

'Believing without believing' means to choose one's own intention and follow it to the end, unshakably. It is a high state of being that can be attained only by men of integrity who know and practice the *Art of Acting—it* demands the elimination of falsehood, and the freedom from the captivity of all superstition and credulity.

For an ordinary man, for those who have not attained an interior unity, believing and not believing are the same lie. To believe is not difficult. Everyone believes in something, but forcing oneself to believe is for the few.

It is not the object of belief that imprisons men, but the believing itself. Atheists, who most people view as people of strength, ones who refuse to lean on the illusory crutch of a God, unlike the rest of humanity, have in reality placed weakness as the common denominator and the very foundation of that doctrine. The atheist has first transferred divinity outside himself, and then denied its existence.

The mortal sin of atheism therefore is not disbelief in God, denial of His existence, but disbelief in oneself.

'The desire to eliminate God by those who call themselves atheists is their attempt, secret even to themselves, to exorcise their fear of death. A fear that grips and torments them more than any other'.

The new humanity will understand that *believing* induces membership to the masses of those who profess faith, the multitude of persons who spend their lives in a state of identification, of belonging, that sticks them to the flypaper of time. Even 'disbelief' in God, as the atheists assert, is a belief that equally sinks them in the *mare magnum* of fundamentalists, dogmatists, the intolerant and ideologues of every persuasion.

Every creed, any faith you choose to embrace enlists you in an army of liars. 'Belief' makes you a follower of the doctrine of lying. You will get stuck in a vicious circle, entrapped in an unnecessary struggle. Spiritual Seekers have transferred the struggle for worldly goods to the struggle for heavenly riches but nothing is changed; they were lying before and they are still lying now. Instead of enjoying the world and laughing, they grunt, blame and complain.

How much better off they'd be, and what greater benefit they'd derive if they'd stop looking for the truth outside and find the lie inside themselves.

Experience will never teach you anything.

It is good to develop roles and personalities that will act and deal with outer reality while early in life, but you should not identify with them and get lost. Soon you must turn all your attention to your inner voice, the real source of all and everything.

Listen to yourself! As soon as there is an atom of knowledge coming from within, you will witness the whole world turning upside down.

When an unpleasant circumstance arises, bring it close to yourself, hold it up to the glow of your inner light and sustain it with your intent. If you can bring it towards yourself and touch that pain, it will dissolve immediately and with it, the outer experience transforms.

Without the friction caused by this work inside, there will be neither sparks nor fire within; you should not avoid it. The fire is that very friction you generate when you face your inner pain. Bring it so close to you that it cannot harm you and in so doing, annul it.

Is there something that escapes you? Look for it in the most hidden corners of your being. No one wants to see. If you give a blind man the vision of an ordinary man, it would be impossible for him to move. He would not adapt. It would be impossible for him to get his bearings. He does not want to see as we do not want to change. In the school, you have to just act your part without believing.

It's the not believing that makes things happen! This is the only way to go through life—to conquer yourself. The ability to believe without believing is the power to contain yourself and not be taken in by either circumstances or events. As soon as you lose the awareness that everything is a projection of yourself, you are at the mercy of your pain—of your unconscious suffering.

I have discovered how to win all the time.

Nothing coming from outside will ever change or help man to achieve any possible evolution and freedom—freedom from the description of the world, from false ideas, from fears, doubts and superstitions, freedom from internal and external pressure. For a man to be completely free, he has to be guided by his own will, self-knowledge and inner understanding.

Be vigilant! To fully possess himself, a man must learn to seek out and touch his inner pain. Everyone is working for you to this end. The world is a beautiful show that you yourself have staged, a marvellous game at your disposal where you are the author of all that happens.

Learn to use it, suffer intentionally, and from the ashes of this fire from within will emerge your will: the very source of all victory and success.

You

If no law of karma, punishment or injustice exist in life, why then is one child born deformed and another perfect? Why does the destiny of one man lead to joy and success and another to failure and destruction? Why does one race live in peace and prosperity and another suffer continual prejudice and persecution?

The Dreamer

Because of you.

When you stop believing in time as something real, these abyssal distances and paradoxical contradictions that you see in the world will cease to exist. Look at things from within and you will realise that there is nobody suffering but you. You are the only sufferer. The apparent law of cause and effect is just a way of thinking. In reality, all is here and now and all is one.

Remember! Whatever is in time is false and cannot explain anything concerning the truth.

'Karma' is just a word invented by man in the attempt to give an explanation to the 'apparent' evil and injustices existing in the world. The law of 'karma' is, for man, another subterfuge to justify his lack of will and freedom.

You only have to know that there is no karma at all that determines the 'great show' of your existence, but only the all-embracing, creative power of now.

You

What's the use of knowing that 'all is here and now and all is one'?

The Dreamer

If you realise this in your body, nothing will ever be impossible to you.

Whatever your state of being is in this moment, this is your past and your future, always and forever.

Just a little self-attention would be enough to solve all the world's problems. But we're always away from 'home' and when we do come 'home', we find it devastated, empty and blame the ghosts.

Remember! The slightest change in your being projects an entirely new world, new history and new destiny.

To all appearances, you wouldn't hesitate to say 'yes' to a new octave in life, to a higher state of being. But as soon as the opportunity presents itself, you take a step backwards, you hesitate. Because in reality, you don't want to change.

Mediocrity has become your home; it protects you, makes you feel safe. If you could listen to yourself, to what you feel and think, to what is really happening inside of you in just this moment, you would realise that this state of being is not something momentary; it is instead what happens within you throughout the whole day, every day of your existence. What you are feeling in this very moment, spreads out in all directions, 360 degrees and is the very root of everything you have been and everything you will ever be.

Identified as you are with the world of appearances, you don't realise that all that keeps you strenuously occupied every day, darkens and imprisons you through thousands of *'small deaths'*, until you finally succeed in materialising the gruesome goal of a physical death.

You wake up in the morning and go into the world begging for a better job, a more successful life, recognition, satisfaction, sex. You study and go to school, work on the computer, go to churches, travel, dance and hold conferences, but you are a sleepwalker like thousands of other shadows.

This disorder appears to you as life. Being tossed around by the world makes you feel busy and useful, but ask yourself: how can something that is virtual and inexistent give you security, offer you a job, make you happy and give you life?

You believe the roles that you are called to act throughout life and use them as an excuse, an alibi to hide yourself, to return into your infernos, in your inner ghettos. You are shadows and want to remain that way.

There is an involuntary will that pushes every man to stay in that inferno.

If you could only 'stop' more often and realise in the flesh, in your body that the world is a projection, something laughable, chaotic, disorderly, you'd dedicate your every breath to understand the real meaning of the 'Art of Acting'. If you could intentionally get rid and dissolve all the external roles that keep you busy and satisfy you, if you could abandon this hypnotic dependence on the world, everything would take on significance and new meaning.

Wealth, prosperity and order would belong to you effortlessly.

Your body would create and emit freedom.

You

Can you explain the difference there is between commitment and identification?

The Dreamer

You can be committed without identifying. This is the way of a man of integrity. You can be identified without commitment and this is the way of most people on earth. Commitment is a vertical way, a new life which transcends itself endlessly.

Identification is a circle which repeats itself and dies. Identification is a mere reaction to something you believe has already happened. Commitment is the creative projection of what is going to happen. Identification is a self-created prison. Commitment is freedom—the sure step of one who knows that as he steps, that path is formed before him. Remember! Whatever you identify with has power over you. Identification means slavery. Be flexible in life and remember your aim—master the art of acting. This is the key to survival.

You cannot become whole in a minute, in a day, in one year or in a lifetime, but just now.

You

How can I be responsible without being worried, or being worried without being responsible?

The Dreamer

You have to learn how to be inertly responsible and at the same time 'acting' impeccably, like a great actor on the stage, the role of being worried, identified or lost when it is necessary, or, in the same way, 'acting' to feel certain, secure or safe when circumstances require to be so, you will be able to create and govern your life and the people and the world around you in a way that only great leaders and remarkable men have been capable to do.

To be responsible, comes from the Latin word *respondere*, which means 'to respond', to 'be answerable'.

To be answerable means that you are not asking anything from the world outside; it means realising that everything is beginning in you, that all comes from within.

Inner responsibility is the action of a warrior that does not allow any fear, doubt or anxiety, to manifest within himself and project outside in the world of events as conflicts, violence and crisis. It is the action of changing the reality without by eliminating the limits within.

It means not blaming and depending upon others, upon the government, upon the weather, upon the politics, upon the economics, upon God. It means saying to yourself: 'I am responsible for all. I am the only one responsible for whatever happens in my life'.

To be responsible means to be always vigilant and alert; to eliminates fear, anger, frustration, guilt, discomfort, overload and inadequacy from your life and to make you live in a state of intelligence and pleasure, so that you can meet any challenge coming on your way as an opportunity to produce fire within and a greater life without.

'Identification is your worst enemy and the greatest evil for humanity'.

People think that identifying or worrying about others will help them but being identified never helps. It is just another way to create your own prison and lose power.

You must realise that being identified is the only emotion that humanity can experience, although they give it many names.

'To act means that there is not one instant in which you are not aware of yourself'.

To be aware of yourself means to contain everyone around you. Can you maintain this awareness, this attention, every moment of your life? If you could do that, you would see everything change; the people, the events—reality itself couldn't be the way you are living it now. You would project a healthier, richer, more unified world.

You will see that the reality outside yourself would become a very good servant; that all that you need will be given to you, because you are responsible for all and everything.

When you master yourself, you are mastering the entire world.

You

What is the fastest way to resolve problems when they arrive?

The Dreamer

To resolve them before they happen.
Problems exist to make you see and touch that which you do not want to see and touch in yourself. If you resolve them inside, they lose their reason for being.
Resolving inside is an act of will, and will reveals itself only after a long work of transformation.

You

How should we approach the daily challenges of running a company or any business? Should we not rely on plans and strategies to ensure their success?

The Dreamer

Wherever you are, whatever you are doing, whether walking or sitting, working or sleeping, you must never stop the precious work of 'remembering your self'.

Every appointment you make and every meeting you arrange serves to strengthen your illusion of being alive, to corroborate yourself in your foolish convictions.

First of all, be able to plan. 'Planning and believing it is like dying. One can only plan what is dead'. The true plan is in this moment, in the 'here and now'. A leader can have armies of collaborators who make plans and programme future operations in every detail, but his own decisions will always be the fruit of the moment.

Until that moment, he neither knows nor does he act until the moment reveals its eternity. Only then will he know what he needs to know. Everything will be at your disposal once you have learned to live the moment in its entirety.

Plans and programmes arise naturally, without effort, when you cease believing in them.

Let the game continue, let the comedy unfold. Allow collaborators and professionals to do what their role demands. The external reality is a theatrical representation, with masks and characters who follow a script. Don't believe it! Don't lose your way! Don't forget that it's just a game.

Win It Before It Happens

'Win it before it happens' is a state of proactivity.

When a problem arises, it is defeat that rears its head as a warning signal of a fault inside, a crack in your being. Go back to the source, and there, in timelessness, you will see that the problem is already resolved.

If you are alive inside, everything will be given to you.

Victory is a state of being you will find only in invisibility…in the timeless suspension when you are neither described nor created by anything but yourself. When you are the creator!

Win it before it happens! To do this, you must pay attention to yourself in every moment and to intervene as soon as you feel pain inside and then just with your attention, remain in the state of victory. When you face someone, you have to contain them. Feel the space around you, and that pain you feel can no longer surround and limit you.

The Creator lives with a sense of dignity. When the Creator arrives, even the atoms know and acknowledge him—the same goes for when you are afraid.

We are deceived by the visible world. You should do everything there is to do, but without expecting gratification from the outside, because even if it comes when you are in a state of expectancy, you will feel vulnerable and afraid of losing it all.

When you have success inside, your state of victory spreads out for 360 degrees.

Remember! The lowest form of vanity is believing to believe. You have to 'do' everything externally without believing in it. The more violent you are inside, the more you occupy the lower levels in the world of opposites: in your job or in the role you play.

By harmonising your inner conflicts, you enter into a state of permanent victory and these will never have to manifest themselves in the world of events.

Who really loves, does not work. Therefore, eliminate all that obstructs this creative 'idleness', and love yourselves inside in order to be victorious…to put the pieces of your fragmented being together, to collect yourself and live a moment of integrity—as state of success.

When looking for an answer, a solution or a creative idea, stop thinking for a moment and focus the entire attention on your inner states and conditions; become aware of the stillness, stay in the realm of pure being for as long as you feel comfortable.

Inner awareness is the supreme creative seed of all and everything.

You have to create and enjoy these moments of calm and solitude and stillness. Otherwise, you will get lost in trying to resolve one conflict after another in the outer world as your inner fragmentation manifests itself.

Believing merely to believe or blindly following something outside yourself, be it the noblest idea or the basest desire, is always identification, and as such, a defeat.

How can your own projection 'elect' you, and how can you desire for your creation to create you? Rely on no one! When you think about this, you feel a sense of freedom arriving. It encroaches uncontrollably, and where before there was an absence, now there is integrity…there is success.

Do you have a problem outside? Win it before it happens!

The Art of Acting at the Times of Lupelius

In the school of Lupelius, difficulties and friction were created artificially to guide disciples to carefully study and observe with attention their own reactions.

Very often, it was necessary to intentionally produce irritation, conflicts and exhaustion so that the work on oneself could have meaning and produce tangible results. It was much more difficult to uncover one's own weaknesses than to see those of others'—to discover in oneself the same faults, limits and errors that were easily accused and despised in the others.

In this way, everyone served as a mirror for someone else to accumulate much information and material to speed up one's own process of integration and perfection.

To train or to put to test the maturity, intelligence and technical mastery of his followers, Lupelius secretly invited legendary warriors and ruthless mercenaries highly skilled in the arts of war.

They would usually present themselves masked as merchants or priests, minstrels and bards, comedians and court jesters, nomads and adventurers, but very often artfully disguised in the role of beggars, tramps, thieves or assassins, who in the right moment, would reveal themselves to be sly, powerful fighters engaged by Lupelius himself to raise the level of understanding, incorruptibility and invincibility of his warrior-monks to enable them to realise the ultimate purpose, the goal of all goals: victory over death.

To Be Is to Not Be

Become a 'no one'.
All things are born from 'nothing'. The closer you get to nothing, the healthier and more successful is your life.
You can be 'someone' only if you become a 'no one'.
And the status of 'nobody' can only be conquered inside.

Being is a not-being!
If there is 'someone', it is only a character in a play, a fleeting shadow on the surface. Inside, there is a no one; the inside is hollow, without contents, pure space.
When you find out who lives in that emptiness, you will laugh. There isn't anyone—there is exactly nothing.
Being is the space within that gives form to everything.
Emptiness or the void is reality, and unless you become 'empty', you will have to suffer because the world of appearance is suffering.
The inner space of a sinner is the same as that of a saint.
In silence, with eyes closed, you will meet your own emptiness—the not-doing that creates and moves everything in the universe.
Don't be afraid of being 'no one'. Only a nobody can be somebody. Entering into the world of nobodiness means becoming 'real'.

A nobody has touched the void within himself and 'knowing nothing', knows everything.

Only a man free from identification can stay alive in a world that demands his total involvement.
You can survive only if you act impeccably the role the circumstances require.

So never stop acting!
Consciously acting is the way to transcend all roles in life and overcome death.

Chapter IV
No War Within, No War Without

When you get rid of all the violence, conflict and misery inside yourself, crimes, revolutions and wars will miraculously disappear from this planet.

*The pain and suffering you meet when you consciously enter into yourself is no less than that which you experience unconsciously every day of your life.
Dive deep within and strive to find out what you are in reality. Only then, you will see your dreary life being transformed in an everlasting, beautiful adventure.*

To change the outer conditions of life, you must change your inner being: the way out is the way in.

Man has a destructive attitude, a ceaseless desire to self-sabotage in the desperate attempt to demonstrate that death really does exist, and like criminality, sickness, poverty and old age, there are forces too powerful for anything to oppose.

Whenever tragedy and disasters strike, you will see in people's faces a grimace of pain. It would seem it was the disaster itself to provoke their reaction and that they had a just cause for which to show their disdain. In reality, it is exactly that cry of pain, that ill feeling that every one of us carries inside that produces not only what we see as a tragedy, but all the mishaps of the planet.

It seems impossible and yet there is no catastrophe, human or natural, that hasn't happened first inside us and then unfolded in the world of events. The absence of integrity of the individual, a lack of self-love, is the real cause of the many disasters, calamities, wars and destruction.

For an ordinary man, there is no pain more painful than the absence of pain. Pain is his daily bread, and war, his permanent inner condition.

To justify our shortcomings and escape from our responsibilities as creators, we've invented a new enemy to fight, even more ferocious and invisible than before: world terrorism. This, unfortunately, can never be overcome if we don't recognise in us its real nature.

Terrorism, in fact, is nothing but a mirror reflection of the fear and violence that we ourselves carry inside.

In order to eliminate war and terrorism from Earth, you need to eliminate the very cause of their existence: your inner conflicts. You have to realise that *you are gods in human form* and therefore you can create health, peace, prosperity and happiness in the same way you created disasters, suffering and death.

Have you ever dreamed a humanity without hunger and without anger, a humanity which lives for the sake of truth, goodness and beauty and not for need?

A world without starving children, without wars, without disease, without poverty? A world dedicated to its own conscious awakening and harmony? Open to new ideas, daring to be different, rising above conformity and mediocrity? A world sustained by light where youthing and physical immortality are normal and natural?

Well! You yourself are called to pave the way!

By forgetting who you really are, you have created a world of appearances, of shadows, of illusions and want to find out the solution out of something that exist only in your imagination. Wake up! And remember! The way out is the way in. Only here, in this very body, through an inner transmutation, you will find the solution to all problems and difficulties.

When you are in the 'now' state of being, you have the power to unify and harmoniously change the course of history: hunger will disappear from the planet if you would only stop believing in your own need of help, poverty will disappear from all people on earth if you would only 'know' how to dissolve your own inner misery; all the shames of politics, religions and ideologies, with their racism and persecutions, will cease to afflict the world once and for all if you would only stop harming yourself inside.

The power of will, once unburied from the most hidden recesses of your being, projects a place where there are no divisions, no boundaries, no conflicts between yourself and the others. Where suffering is, your inner blindness is its very cause, and where conflict is, your misery is its very root. Your healing is their healing and your inner victory, the salvation of the entire world.

Remember! When tremendous vicissitudes and calamities come, don't panic! Be still and for a few minutes, stand perfectly quietly. Move all your attention from anything happening outside or disturbing you, and watch yourself.

Watching yourself is the key to all solutions; knowing that all comes from within and simultaneously materialises itself in the world of events, you are afraid to look inside, to be aware of anything dark or negative that happens within, believing that your attention could amplify or fix it in your being and make it last forever. But you forget that any negative state disappears the very moment you become aware of it.

Watching yourself moves from within all your misery and agony of despair. It lifts your being above the storm, the wreckage and disasters that life apparently seems to create. Watching yourself silently turns you into a living dynamo of incredible power, capable of transforming any trouble, disaster or challenge into a miraculous victory.

You have to find out what pure observation or pure seeing is. You have to find out how to go beyond time, which means how to get rid of inner dialogue, criticism, judging, liking or disliking, accusing, condemning—self-observation makes you attentive, vigilant and in that attention, all sense of the past and future disappears, and with it, all concepts, images and descriptions will dissolve.

'You may ask for freedom, for truth or happiness, but not see how factors that govern your being, such as the love of your negative states, your grievances, your secret jealousies, your laziness, your inner considering, your fears, your doubts, your dislikes and so on, are asking for something very different, and that your inner power is going to realise all that you are secretly willing and unconsciously projecting'.

Learn to be still.

You've spent so many years making do with only the most marginal results that success for you is as foreign as colour to a blind man or pure oxygen to a sea urchin.

You consume your energy in useless activities, in uneasiness, in anxiety and negative imagination until you are exhausted and therefore can justify the sense of defeat you know so well. You think that if you succeed in avoiding the vibration of transformation which you so wrongly call discomfort, pain and even hunger, that you have accomplished something—when in fact, you've only succeeded in killing your body's own life impulse, and eliminated your only chance.

Learn to be still. Seek the quiet inside, not through violence or force, but through comprehension. Every voice within you cries out to be heard and calls for attention; your ignorance will only constrain them to silence but their needs persist regardless.

Observe yourself within!

Self-observation will show you that you have no control of your thoughts and emotions, and that they come and go whether you wish them or not. And it is the same with your feelings, and with your moods, and your words and your actions.

Through self-observation, you will realise that you are not one but many, that you are not a whole but a multitude and that that very fragmented being is the real cause of all your troubles, difficulties and illnesses.

Through self-observation, you will realise that the world outside is an empty screen on which you project the shadows of a disintegrated psychology.

Once you realise that it all comes from within, that the world in which you live is not projected onto you…but by you, your fear will come to an end. And when fear is gone, a new world, a new life, never conceived before, will appear before your very eyes.

Remember! Your mission in life is to touch the unexplainable in you, the unknown, to become one with your dream. You must never lose sight of this.

No development of inner integrity, no power of doing is possible without the transformation of negative emotions and suffering.

By struggle and only by struggle, your being can be transformed.

Conscious attention to the breath and intentional enduring of suffering can evoke in you such a powerful, inexplicable experience of joy and freedom. Remember! Without suffering, you have no fire for transformation. You need fire for your understanding and growth.

You have to find the strength and endurance that enables you to suffer gladly, and suffer without suffering.

You

Do you mean that the war in Iraq, and the war in Afghanistan, all terror attacks and religious fanaticisms, the Arab-Israeli conflict and all crimes and horrors in the world are happening because of me?

The Dreamer

Those wars are not outside but within you. Those wars, as any war, never really happened in time but only in your imagination, that's why you are at the same time responsible for and victim of a world that you yourself project and believe to be real.

Remember! There is no war, and there is no peace in the world. War and peace exist only in your imagination.
War is a state of being! And only you yourself have the power to either create or stop it.
No war within, no war without.

You

And the people who are finding themselves right now in the middle of a conflict or war, what fault do they have?

The Dreamer

It is impossible to find yourself in a war if you don't produce death within yourself or if you don't dream of it.

War, poverty, failure, disease, death or any other disaster are not objective realities. They are not outside yourself. They become real only if you dream of them. To be a politician, you have to produce conflicts, within and without, although you pretend to fight for peace. To be a journalist, you have to produce scandals, and first of all, within yourself. That's why your life is a catastrophe. To be a doctor, you have to materialise illnesses and viruses, the same ones that one day will kill you.

The economy of your energy-body is the key to physical health and world's justice, peace and prosperity. Everything outside yourself is but an imagined fragmented mirror of your inner being.

Through self-mastery and self-knowledge, an individual can liberate the entire humanity from its state of war and conflicts, from the slavery of the work, from the corruption of politics, from the tyranny of financial oppression, and one day from the dependency on machines, computers and robots.

War, like poverty, is not an objective status, but a subjective state of being.

War, like poverty, is an inner matter and never an outer reality. The world in its apparent objectivity is only a projection. War, poverty, horrors, disease and death are only within. They all come from within, are a reflection of your subjectivity, and only you can heal and save the world if you know how to heal and save yourself.

Trying to gain peace through war, or to eliminate war through peace is the presumption of a childish humanity trapped in a game of suffering and death from which there is no escape.

When you can live in the absence of time, when you can return to your integrity, you can harmoniously unify the course of history; you can make hunger disappear from the world, make diseases no longer afflict people, make all the political religious and ideological atrocities with their racism and persecutions, cease to manifest in the world instantly.

You believe your mission on earth to be to love each other and help others, but how can you help the world if you are the very cause of its tragedy and misery? The only way you can help the world is to wake up from this nightmare. The world incarnates your very being; it is just the replica of all that you are. If you were really concerned about the world, you would abandon your daily routines and afflictions and enter into a state of self-awareness from which alone you can really help.

Remember! There is no evil more harmful than the lie of helping someone else, and no illusion more deadly than expecting someone's help. Stop asking for help and the world will stop being in need! Stop being in need and the world will cease to ask for help! There is no one 'out there' to help and no god in heaven who can help you. It's all up to you.

The world is such because you are such; no one and nothing needs help but your vanity, your protagonism, your lying that seeks to survive at all costs. The need to help others is the real cause of all misery, injustice and violence.

The only help you can give to others is to free yourself from the need to help.

One day, you'll realise that no human disasters, injustice or natural calamities are really happening on earth but just in yourself and not even that: What is really happening in yourself, that is, in your body, is a sort of identification with an illusory, tiny bubble of nothing.

In a man, when the level of inner righteousness lowers, disasters, injustice and natural calamities increase.

You

How should we react then, to all the sufferings and bloodshed in this world? To the thousands of people overwhelmed by floods and the millions dying of starvation?

The Dreamer

That too is part of that illusory description that you call reality. What you have to do then, is to recognise it not as something happening externally, but within yourself and let it be. This will make you real and the world safe.

Sorrow in the world is due to your having forgotten your own being, having given reality to the picture on the screen.

This world can be changed if you work on yourself. Causes or no causes, you have made this world and you can change it. The reason why you don't understand is because you believe that you are in the world and not that the world is in you. Taking appearance for reality is a mortal error and the very cause of all calamities.

The very cause of all natural calamities and human disasters is your conflictual inner being. In an external disaster, only those who refuse to understand will be destroyed. Your inner states and attitudes determine whether the great cycles of nature are going to kill you or take you to a new dimension, to a higher level of understanding where all human horrors, diseases, wars, poverty and death, will cease to exist.

You

What about the media? Are they not telling us what in the world is really happening? Are they not telling us the truth about the conditions of the people in the world?

The Dreamer

No! They are only telling you about your inner states and conditions. They are only telling you what you want them to tell you.

You
Are you then saying that everything that we see and read in the news is false?

The Dreamer
Not only is it false, because 'false' is a distortion of what is real...but it has never happened—it is your pure fantasy and invention.

You

What shall we do then? Stop reading and watching the news altogether?

The Dreamer

Continue to read and listen to them as before, but conscious of the fact that all that stuff is not coming from the world outside but from your own dark, compromised inner being trapped like a spider in its own web.

Learn then, to discern. Learn how to believe without believing. Learn how to exorcise your self-fulfilling prophecy of disaster. Learn how to laugh at your own deadly creativity and act your role in life as an actor does on a movie-set, impeccably and intentionally, without ever forget that behind all this performance, there is you yourself—the Dreamer—creator, sustainer and transformer of all and everything.

Immorality means self-forgetfulness.
Immorality means self-harmfulness.

Only you yourself can be immoral and harm yourself by forgetting what you are. When you remember yourself, all troubles and difficulties disappear from the planet. The world is made in your image; it reflects your inner being and obeys any of your commands, whatever they may be.

When you stop suffering, the entire world ceases to be immoral.

Be free from the influence of every form of hypnotism, dependence, superstition or identification with the world.

Do not lean on anybody's knowledge, fantasy or prophecy.

Know that there is no power 'out there' that can destroy you.

'Out there', nothing can happen without your consent, inner approval or intent.

Be vigilant! Cast off all your ignorance and darkness. It is your vision that needs some adjustment and not humanity's.

If you integrate yourself, if you become a unity, then the world is safe.

In the world of duality, everything is perfectly balanced: a period of obscurity and destruction inevitably alternates with a period of creativity and constructiveness, but only as a mirror of your inner states.

So don't worry about the world, worry only about yourself, this is the only way you can help. The world of events and circumstances is totally depending upon you.

The conditions of the world correspond exactly to your inner states.

Remember! Nobody and nothing can do anything if it is not commanded and directed by your own dream.

No war within, no war without; this is the law.

What's 'Fair' and What's 'Unfair'

An entire family being slaughtered in the middle of the night without any reason, pulling the plug on a dying man in the name of euthanasia, a dictator, merciless assassin, responsible for the death of thousands, being sentenced to death, a flood wiping away entire villages and thousands of people… What's 'fair' and what's 'unfair'?

Remember! Everything under the jurisdiction of time is false.

Time Magazine, The Chronicle, 60 Minutes, Russia Today, CNN, BBC, Sole 24 Ore, the New York Times, World News Tonight, all instruments of time and communicators of death that, you yourself have produced for your own entertainment; an amusing comedy, an extraordinary game that you yourself have turned into a concentration camp, creating history to delineate a territory of death and marking its boundaries with your memory as a wild animal does with urine.

Apparently, memory gives you certainty and security, but like all that which has a beginning and an end, a birth and a death, it will leave you sooner or later in the middle of nowhere.

What a fantasy! What an imagination! What a performance!

All that which is history, all that which is time, all that which is memory has never happened and can never happen except in your imagination. History is a nightmare that you impose on yourself to justify your lack of will and freedom, and perpetuate your own limits, fear, forgetfulness and death.

History is an addiction you would never know how to live without!

When you remember that all comes from within and that whatever has happened in your life is only a sad projection of your inner fragmentation and lack of will, you will have the power to give the right command to your body, to transfer inner integrity and understanding to your cells. And in doing so, your external world, the world that you call reality, will only know peace and prosperity, and be governed by harmony, intelligence and justice.

Exercise your inner integrity and the world will stop being conflictual.
Exercise your inner prosperity and poverty will disappear from this planet.
Exercise your immortality and you will not see death anymore.

Learn to discern. Learn how to believe without believing, learn how to exorcise your self-fulfilling prophecy of disaster; learn how to laugh at your own deadly negative imagination.

You
So can war ever be stopped? Can there be salvation for the world?

The Dreamer
Which world do you want to save? The world of your projections? Of your own nightmares? Of your own despair? Get rid of the belief that people need your help and see whether there is anything left to save.

War will cease to exist the moment you 'stop believing' that war is outside yourself.

You

If there is a God or a higher being governing the universe, why does He not make this Earth a peaceful place to live with enlightened human beings that love and trust each other unconditionally?

The Dreamer

Look at yourself, study yourself and you will know the answer. You are not a unity but a multitude, a legion, a multiplicity. Inside yourself, you are a crowd of negative people fighting each other, full of negative states which destroy your own happiness and make you miserable and ill. This is why the world appears to you as a theatre of horrors, cruelty and wars.

There is no God to blame but only yourself.

The world needs neither redeemers nor saviours. Those who want to redeem the world are the real carriers of all evil. How could they cure the ills of the world if they themselves don't know to be the very cause?

The world is as you dream it and cannot be otherwise. The job of a redeemer is hard. Sooner or later, he remains victim of the very ones he believes to be saving. The world, being your mirrored image, knows much more than what you know about yourself. It knows all that you don't want to see and touch within. It knows every single weakness and conflict. And more than anything else, it knows about your harmful activity that you impose upon your being. Remember! The outer world is the faithful unfolding of an inner pattern that you yourself set in motion.

You must know how to use the fire inside you if you want to change your inner hell into a paradise. This fire is the conscious suffering, without which it is impossible to create anything. You must be aware of what makes you suffer and, once recognised, learn to use it.
The intentional suffering is the conscious acceptance of the suffering of all humanity, in all its forms, as your own.

When you learn to transform your inner pain in this precious substance, the whole world will be freed from all the suffering and all its horrors. Pay always attention to the evil inside you and the world will live in harmony and justice.

Love yourself ceaselessly. It's not a person or an external event that menaces your life, but your recurring ignorance—your fears that reincarnate themselves. Don't accuse the others or the world for your suffering. Look at yourself inside and make an effort to separate yourself from these countless daily deaths, this useless, painful self-sabotage that is the cause of all evil.

Innocence is the way out. Innocence means to stop dying within.
In a man when the level of inner righteousness lowers, human disasters, injustice and natural calamities, increase.

This is because you are always creating the reality you see and touch, even if in a state of complete unwariness. You fail to recognise the world as the perfect reflection of what you are, and get frightened when confronted with it.

But the world is as you dream it.

You have to remove the ballast of negative emotions and thoughts in order to get closer to the most real part of yourself. Go deep within and let your inner being give way to innocence; go all the way in and dig out the buried will, the lost integrity, the dream that creates and transforms.

Be a seeker, become a hunter! In the morning, listen to your song of sorrow made of fears, doubts and guilt. Do not escape. That's the battlefield. Do not leave home without winning, without having regained a state of certainty and unity.

You

But how shall we act when the others wrong us? When we are victim of an injustice?

The Dreamer

All your life you've been told about defending your rights…to decisively react to any insult or attack…to stand up for yourself…to speak your mind and let your voice be heard, without ever realising that these are all lies and that true freedom is the right to NOT react…and the true revolution—the conscious effort to remain still.

While a battle rages inside you, have the strength to stay there, within and not identify with anything going on outside. By simply 'doing nothing', you will win all battles without ever fighting.

In stillness, secretly and silently, victory reveals and a new earth, a new heaven, a new life will appear before you very eyes.

It is only 'apparently' that a man confronts external obstacles, or meets enemies and adversaries outside himself. In reality, the antagonist is always the materialisation of a shadow, a dark part of ourselves that we neither know nor want to know.

When it finally manifests itself in the form of an attack, adversity or a problem, we are taken by surprise. In reality, we have unconsciously cultivated it within ourselves; because of our inattentiveness, a tiny symptom has had time to become acute, and due to our inability to identify it and intervene, it has materialised into a real threat.

But you cannot be attacked or persecuted by anything or anyone if you don't perceive yourself as attacked or persecuted fist, if you are not already victim of your own dreary imagination.
It is your very reaction to being persecuted that in return, is creating and projecting persecutions in the outer world; your inner conflicts and self-sabotage that are more dangerous than any war.

Remember! The victim is always guilty!
The weak will disappear only if you recognise your inner weaknesses; and the meek, the poor and the victims of all atrocities will disappear only if you are conscious of your inner harmfulness, misery and conflicts.

It is your division that creates the violence that you then meet outside, because the world is such because you are such!
The world is as you dream it—accidents, criminality and death are the results of a long series of inner crimes.
So, stop lying to yourself, and the world will show you all its goodness, truth and beauty.
It is the recognition of an inner causality—the being responsible for all that happens outside, that makes evil, sufferings and death totally disappear from earth.

You

Don't you think that the real facts are right under our nose: the horrors of war, the suffering of refugees, the poverty in many countries, religious strife and separation, economic and social injustice, hatred and every form of corruption in the world?

The Dreamer

What you believe to be real facts are just the outer expressions of an alchemical phenomenon which is happening, right now, within you and nowhere else. By believing that all this is happening outside yourself, you have been forced to find external solutions to the endless problems of the world. But all your efforts, all your strategies to change the world—from political reforms and revolutions to a religious, spiritual life of denial and solitude, from a life of sacrifice and discipline to the social fights for the recognition of human rights—revealed themselves to be a failure.

You have tried so many things, even being sincere and honest with yourself, but without being able to focus your attention on the real cause of all this confusion: your inner fragmentation and deaths.

You

But how do we apply such vision in a world of human fear, uncertainty and evil? How do we apply such theory to Nations politically corrupted, States and countries up for a long time in international conflicts? How do we apply such view to a world where warfare and terror persist? Is it possible to adopt and apply a moral approach in an immoral world, a spiritual consciousness to a material, practical world?

The Dreamer

All evils and boundaries are the apparent effect of an imaginary division between yourself and the world; that means that only you yourself through an inner transformation and understanding can put an end to this collective self-hypnotism and madness.

Master yourself and you will liberate the world from all evils.

The individual will heal the world.

You

Then can you tell me how to deal with these negative emotions? And how to get rid of them?

The Dreamer

Negative emotions are not the problem. Ignoring or misunderstanding them is. In order to eliminate negative emotions, you must first be fully aware of them. Observe what happens when you are negative. Notice how everything falls in the wrong place within you. Notice how much you lie and justify in negative moods and how dark everything appears to your eyes. On the other side, if you are aware of it, instantly everything changes and you'll feel charged with an incredible energy and vitality. Give attention to your inner states whatever they are. Through earnestness and patience, you will discover something very precious and very powerful that hides behind their apparent unpleasantness.

Be consciously aware of your thoughts and they will die by themselves. If you are there, nothing else can be. If you are aware even for few minutes a day, your lifestyle will change and your actions will reflect your clarity, your silence, your grace.

Fearlessly, dive deep within and draw closer to your negative states. The light of your awareness will make them disappear, and allow you to experience the summit of perfection and integrity as a permanent state.

When your being is trained to truth and become whole, your thoughts, words and actions automatically will lose the power to hurt and wound, and your voice can be heard among the gods, for you have overcome death.

You

After many failed attempts, I realised that happiness on earth is impossible and that everything that surrounds us constantly feeds this unhappiness. I am aware of this and do not know how to change.

The Dreamer

You say you are aware of your unhappiness, but do not know how to intervene. But how can you be aware and unhappy at the same time?

Unhappiness comes from unawareness, from self-forgetfulness, and so does all evil.

If you were aware and totally present, all darkness would dissolve instantly. To keep your own misery alive, you have to feed it with time. Time is its lifeblood. Remove time through the self-awareness and all the difficulties and sufferings that apparently surround you, will disappear. It is through a silent but intense battle against 'forgetting yourself' that unhappiness will die. You're here to be a warrior, you are not searching for inner peace; a warrior does not seek peace, but the battle and fight. Chase the war in yourself, as a predator does with its prey. This is your mission: observing your inner war.

You

What do you suggest we have to sacrifice in order to reach a higher level of understanding?

The Dreamer

In this work, there is only one thing you can and have to sacrifice, and that is your suffering. Here, you learn how useless suffering is. Here, you learn that there is no method, nor system, neither religion nor ideology that can help you to release it. You have to do it all by yourself and from within.

You

What is the real cause of suffering?

The Dreamer

Your identification with the limited, your addiction to thinking and your identification with the outer events. Beware of 'identification', of not remembering! Identification means forgetting, and losing the full authorship of a Dreamer, to annul yourself in the created, to become the dreamed, cheated by your own creations, prisoner of the shadows and at the mercy of events.

But remember, there are no external causes to your suffering, for nothing is external.

Identification or emotional involvement with the world is the silent, invisible cause of all suffering and a mortal attempt to your own happiness.

If you can remain firm, unattached and not identify with what happens in life, you will have the power to move mountains.

There is no suffering in the world but the one you harbour inside.

Grief and pain are nothing more than the materialisation of your lack of responsibility and understanding.

What you call the world is merely the projection of your entire being and what you call pain is the marking of your inner separation.

As you are, only pain can bring you back to the source. Only pain can show you what you are 'missing', but you are so used to it by now that you no longer can live without.
To move a grain of sand in the world of events, you have to turn the entire universe upside down.

You have to transform into light and life every single part of your body, knowing that this fanciful universe with its infinity is none other than a pale reflection of an atom of your body.

You

You say, "Nothing is external!" Then how can you explain that if something keeps me from breathing, I die?

The Dreamer

Nobody and nothing could ever stop you from breathing unless you are subdued by the hypnotic, mortal description of the world.

The world is built by your very breath. As you breathe, so breathes the world. Breathing belongs to you and comes from you and not from 'out there'. Your understanding of breathing is upside-down because you keep telling yourself a backwards tale.

If you stop breathing, it is not you who's going to die but the world outside, your reflection, your shadow.

Then be conscious of this: breathing is an inner power and doesn't depend on anything outside yourself, not even on oxygen.

Difficult to understand, but it is your breathing that makes the world alive, it's your breath that gives life to the entire universe.

Remember! Real life comes from within and nobody and nothing can ever destroy it from outside.

Be constantly aware of the war within, this is the very engine of your development and success.

The refusal to recognise your inner conflict leads to misery and failure.

The Titanic Task

If you want to change something in your life, you have to face the titanic task of abandoning your inner suffering and realise that you yourself are the only cause of all your troubles and difficulties.

To do that, you have to isolate yourself internally and not let outer events crush you: practice non-identifying and self-awareness in all moments and circumstances.

Remember! Your role in life, whatever it is, is perfectly mirroring your inner conditions and mercilessly revealing your level of responsibility. If you realise this, your inner understanding and freedom will expand and with them, your 'power of doing'.

To increase your power of doing, you have to struggle against your love of being negative. To increase your power of doing, you have to make room to your inner light.

Your inner light is the very cause of all that which takes form in the world of events and has to be renewed every day through self-observation, through self-love and understanding.

When pain comes, don't try to interpret it, don't try to change it, or to go beyond or to be free of it. Just be totally aware of it.

Pain can only exist in time. If you observe the pain very attentively, the boundaries of time will fall.

To be aware means to look or to listen without any judgement or criticism, that means to look without all the conditionings of the one who is in pain; without his fears, his anxieties, his worries, and enter into a totally different vision-dimension: Timelessness.

Intentional enduring of the unavoidable suffering, such as the death of someone you love, can evoke in you such a powerful, inexplicable experience of self-mastery and joy.

Out of suffering: joy.

The Perfect Joy

The story told by Francis of Assisi is emblematic to make clear what constitutes the psychological revolution that a man must accomplish to be able to break free from the hypnotic description of an external world.

It is the story of an *Inner Creative Victory*. It is the announcement of the birth of a new man, healed from pain, from doubt, from conflict.

'If when we shall arrive at St Mary of the Angels, all drenched with rain and trembling with cold, all covered with mud and exhausted from hunger; if, when we knock at the convent-gate, the porter should come angrily and ask us who we are; if, after we have told him, "We are two of the brethren," he should answer angrily, "What ye say is not the truth; ye are but two impostors going about to deceive the world, and take away the alms of the poor; begone I say!" If then he refuse to open to us, and leave us outside, exposed to the snow and rain, suffering from cold and hunger till nightfall—then, if we accept such injustice, such cruelty and such contempt with patience, without being ruffled and without murmuring, believing with humility and charity that the porter really knows us, and that it is God who maketh him to speak thus against us, write down, O Brother Leo, that this is perfect joy. And if we knock again, and the porter come out in anger to drive us away with oaths and blows, as if we were vile impostors, saying, "Begone, miserable robbers! To the hospital, for here you shall neither eat nor sleep!" And if we accept all this with patience, with joy and with charity, O Brother Leo, write that this indeed is perfect joy. And if, urged by cold and hunger, we knock again, calling to the porter and entreating him with many tears to open to us and give us shelter, for the love of God, and if he come out more angry than before, exclaiming, "These are but importunate rascals, I will deal with them as they deserve." And taking a knotted stick, he seize us by the hood, throwing us on the ground, rolling us in the snow and shall beat and wound us with the knots in the stick; if we bear all these injuries with patience and joy, thinking of the sufferings of our Blessed Lord, which we would share out of love for him, write,
O Brother Leo, that here, finally, is perfect joy.'

(The Little Flowers of St Francis, chap VIII)

The intensity of this parable is unfathomable. The story of Francis is one of the most valuable documents of humanity. His journey from Perugia through one winter's night, in the mud, in the cold and rain, the offense and the refusal to receive him in his own convent, do not happen in the world of speculation, but in a real virtual reality.

Francis immersed in a simulated situation, which he created, and tested its impeccability. True success is not consensus, the admiration of others, the assertion of superiority, and not even the miraculous things that you can dissolve but something bigger; a treasure that neither thieves nor rust can purloin: your own integrity.

Man is governed by negative emotions to which he is particularly related and with which he identifies, getting lost in a sea of suffering. Circumscribing this condition is the purpose of this work. If you turn your attention towards yourself and for few seconds are aware of what happens within, you will realise that you do not belong to that multitude of thoughts and emotions, but finally to yourself. You cease to be an abstraction, confused and conditioned by inner negative states and become a unity, an individual, a powerful wholeness finally free from the slavery of identification.

No one can set you free but yourself. Try to touch the most painful sensation within yourself to realise that all sufferings are unnecessary and that only intentional suffering, that is *suffering without suffering*, can reveal all the beauty and goodness of your very nature.

Don't try to find any freedom in the world of events, you will be disappointed and get lost. The only freedom that you need to look for is the one from 'identification' with the ballast and mess that you carry inside. Real work is based on the transformation of the inner inferno in 'something' that is still completely unknown to man.

New sciences, new technologies and new religions have nothing to do with this transformation. What we call the new humanity, the technological age and the apparent new discoveries will never transform an atom of man's inner consciousness.

A man who recognises this is ready to escape from his own self-created prison. The gateway to freedom cannot be recognised by those who do not know anything about the Art of Dreaming.

The way to escape is upwards.

Do not react!
Your reaction is the very cause of all that you are reacting to.

You

But why suffer at all? Wouldn't it be a more righteous, fulfilling way to seek to overcome and abandon suffering altogether as Buddhism and other ancient schools teach us?

The Dreamer

You need fire! Without fire, you will never achieve anything. And this fire comes out of suffering, intentional suffering, without which it is impossible to create anything.

So, instead of avoiding, suppressing or eliminating the emotions of suffering, you must intentionally endure the fire that arises from that experience. You must know what makes you suffer and how to make use of it—how to transform it into that fire which, from within, will cook, cement, crystallise and... DO. Suffer off your fears! Suffer off your worries and doubts! Suffer off your anxieties, your pride, your egoism! When you realise that this patient enduring of suffering is a vehicle towards victory over death, then you may find the strength and the humility that enables you to suffer gladly, that is suffer without suffering.

Out of this fire will arise freedom, strength, love, joy, integrity and awe, and transform your unnecessary suffering into the most remarkable power of doing.

You

What should be my attitude toward the present upsetting social conditions, political intrigues and injustices in my country?

The Dreamer

Right now, don't pay any attention at all to them.

Just dedicate your time and energy to your own inner transformation. The injustice you feel in the world is an illusion. The injustice that you see is not coming from outside but from all the poison you carry within. One day, you will realise that the very cause of all poverty, violence and political crimes, which you claim your country to be the victim of, is merely a manifestation of the fragmentation of your own inner being, the projection of a mental disease which can be healed only when you recognise yourself as the only one responsible.

The moment you yourself become an inseparable 'wholeness', your country will be completely free from all tyranny, misery and war.

You will never see a war, because war like poverty is not an objective status but a subjective state of being. War like poverty is an inner matter and never an outer reality.

War, poverty, horrors, disease and death are only within. They all come from within.

What you believe to be an objective world, is only a reflection of your subjectivity; then only you can heal and save the world when you know how to heal and save yourself.

The path to travel takes the form of its traveller.

All evils are the apparent effect of an imaginary division between yourself and the world. Master yourself and you will liberate the world from all evils.

Evil doesn't exist. EVIL is unconsciousness, lack of light, lack of knowledge. Its opposite is LIVE. Evil is life, self-awareness, self-knowledge and light turned upside down.

The most difficult and painful moments are opportunities to penetrate in an area of power. When you feel that pain inside, don't run away from it; stop! There, in stillness, is where you need to stay. Without the ability to grasp these opportunities and live moments of suspension, you will exist in a continual state of identification; existence bends and degrades, and in time, without realising it, you find yourself indulging and repeating the same meaningless life of billions of *people-machines* before you.

When you are in pain, do not touch the world! Stay still and listen! The world has the ungrateful task of telling you all the truth and nothing but the truth. 'Out there', you'll find only something or someone waiting for you to denounce your misery and defeat. The world is your specular creation. You have created it in your image and perfection, and this means that no compromise, no deviation, no gap, no division is allowed between you and your 'reflected image'.

You must realise that the world, acknowledging you as the sole creator and Dreamer of its own existence, in order to denounce its subjugation to sorrow, misery and suffering, cannot do anything other than express loudly and with all its might, the torture, corruption, crime and death that you're imposing upon your inner being twenty-four hours a day!

In order for victory and success to be continuous, you must eliminate every form of conflict from inside. The Dreamer has brought you the most advanced technology for living a life without opposites, a life from which war and sickness have been eliminated. Impose happiness, integrity, beauty and the joy of living upon yourself.

This is the secret to unceasing happiness, to never-ending victory and success, because it continually transcends itself.

But you are divided inside, and your thinking is conflictual, and because of this, you do not know how to live in a world without opposites and antagonists. Believing that the world is a separate reality from you, that inside and outside are in opposition and unrelated to each other, you accept pain, unhappiness and defeat as your natural destiny.

This is why you do not know stillness—condemned as you are to be in constant movement, permanently conditioned by the disaster you carry inside. In stillness, which is the real root of every action, and alone with yourself, you can finally flush out that pain which you carry inside. That pain, not recognised and not circumscribed, broods in a rift in the being and is the real cause of all your failures.

Remember! There is no injustice, no violence, no crime, no war in the world, but in yourself.

Whether good or bad, you are dreaming and creating your reality in this very moment. All is in your hands. All is up to you. Everything comes to the meaning that you give it.

You

I live a comfortable life. I have saved enough to provide for my family, and I am content with what I have. Why should I concern myself with the state of the world, or finding the cause of all its wars and conflicts within me?

The Dreamer

If you don't dare to win your inner war, even what you believe you own will attack you.

If you do not enter into a state of fearlessness, and remain prey of your fragmented psychology, whatever you possess will get smaller and smaller until it vanishes.

There isn't one moment that your life is not at risk!

You

But such is the course of the world, that you have no command over it, nor is it ever subject to you.

If the world is so insubordinate to you, then why should you be so concerned or feel responsible for something so deaf to any command, so loath to any change?

The Dreamer

You justify your impotence towards external events by denying your negative emotions and clothe them with excuses such as complaining about the 'others', the weather, the government, the world-events thus projecting on them all that you don't want accept as being in yourself.

Remember! The outer and the inner are one and the same, and you cannot escape this law.

In front of you, the roll of time unfolds itself and actualises the inevitable 'you'.

You are asking now: What can I do?

You can change the course of events by changing yourself: your inner states and attitude. This is what really matters.

The law of oneness reigns supreme.

You

I try to apply the Dreamer's principles to me in life; whenever a problem arises, I try to observe the reactions within myself, but I often find this exercise to be unbearable. When focused upon, everything appears even more threatening, and the problem seems to worsen.
Why do all my efforts seem to produce no effect?

The Dreamer

You have to realise that self-observation is not supposed to improve your life but mostly to make it worse, and this for the sole purpose of making you aware of all the limits and conflicts you carry inside.

Being an observer, a witness of your inner condition will either increase your stubborn determination to change, allowing you to enter into a higher order of responsibility, or on the contrary, reinforce your reluctance for any change and hurl you back into the infernal jaws of time.

*You asked to be closer to the Dreamer and this doesn't
allow you to do anymore what you used to do,
not even think or feel what you used to think and feel.*

*Living close to the Dreamer, to apply his principles,
is for few and it is very risky.*

*Living close to the Dreamer is the most difficult task
you could ever undertake.*

*Here, if you forget yourself, you will be instantly
catapulted in your dangerous past and get lost.*

*Here, close to the Dreamer, there is no space for you to indulge in any weakness,
regret, doubt and fear.*

Here, you have to be strong!

Here, close to the Dreamer, you can only be pure and whole.

You Should Only Ever Win

How can you rise above ordinary life and all its nonsense and madness?

You need a new vision. When your vision is no longer that of an ordinary man who sees only by opposites—light and dark, right and wrong, good and evil—then and only then, can you rise above the sea of troubles and opposition that affect your life, and witness the world mirror, your inner permanent victory.

This is your nature. Victory is a permanent state of being:

You can only ever win!

'Real victory' like success, has no opposite. The average man has remained victim of a very dangerous virus which has devoured his true memory, the vertical memory, the one that allows him to go back to his miraculous wonder of now.

Therefore, he has forgotten his creative power of dreaming. He projects into the world of events his fragmented, scattered being and has made of duality his own god. This is why man is governed by the 'inner war of opposites' and accepts this condition as his own nature, that a victory is followed by a defeat, success by failure and birth is ineluctably followed by death.

Your world, until you eliminate every form of conflict from inside, will still remain a very threatening and alien place to live: conflictual, precarious and dangerous.

Ordinary man goes through life believing that he deserves heaven while drowns face down in the puddle of his own reflection. He believes to 'own' the world and be in command while he is himself merely a foggy projection of his fading dream.

Remember! What you really 'own', can never be taken from you.

Your greatest task in life is to find out what that is.

When you win the antagonist inside, you will no longer have to meet him outside. He will disappear from your world and everything will lead to your success. Carry these principles in your heart, day and night, and you will know only victory. Victory is the natural state of mankind.

If you are here, it is in order to go beyond, to do incredible things, accomplishments which others consider impossible. So do not waste time doing or copying that which has already been done. Search for the thing that you truly love, that unique, original thing for which you were born.

The world is you. The world lives everything that you live.

The Dreamer has brought you a new technology capable of eliminating war, poverty, old age, sickness and death. You can do it in this very instant! To do it, you must take the world on your shoulders, like the Greek myth of Atlas. You must take responsibility for making all suffering disappear from the world, including death. Impose freedom, integrity and beauty upon yourself—this is the secret to unceasing happiness, to never-ending victory and success… When you know that you are the origin of everything, you also know that every evil eliminated on the inside also disappears from the outside. Only a warrior knows that the world is his reflection and he can intentionally reach such a state of innocence.

The world suffers because you suffer.

So *don't waste your life trying to change the world* from the outside. *Start with you! Change is an inside-out process.* The way you are in this very instant is spreading out in all directions, creating simultaneously what you have been and what you will be.

But man is a prisoner in a self-created prison. He has one freedom—to count his steps inside his cell, but he never dreams of escaping it. Leaving this prison would be more painful than staying in captivity. It takes courage to abandon the world's description and rebel against its diabolical project of ageing, getting sick and dying.

You create failure and defeat. Confusion, doubt, fear of not succeeding—and you live these things inside, even if you don't know it. Mankind secretly loves suffering, defeat and even poverty and sickness. *You have it, because you love it.*

One day, when all fears are gone, you'll never believe that there was something you could be afraid of.

In a state of fearlessness, nothing can scare you, because you'll have no idea of what fear means. For you, fear has never existed. And if someone tried to explain it to you, you will not understand what he is talking about.

When you realise that it is your 'no' attitude that creates the world outside you, that world will no longer have power over you. You will be master of your emotions, and life will become a paradise on earth. When you have eliminated all doubt, right down to the last atom, and filled your whole being with a sense of permanent victory, the world can do nothing but reflect it. This state of completeness, this totality of being is what Christianity calls faith.

Remember! Act in a winning manner when the evidence of defeat is all around you. Act as if you were in possession of victory just for a moment, and then the next moment and the next, and you will see reality miraculously transformed in a permanent victory before your very eyes.

The one who recognises the imperfect as imperfect… is perfect.

The one who is conscious of his inner limits… is limitless.

The one who is aware of his inner fragmentation… becomes whole.

The one who is conscious of his inner conflicts… wins all battles he finds on his way.

Through self-observation, more awareness and more understanding comes into your life.

The moment you realise you are not present… you are present.

The moment you're able to really observe something negative in yourself…you are no longer trapped by it.

The moment you acknowledge yourself to be in pain…the entire world will be liberated from all crime, war and sufferings.

This is not spirituality; it's the Art of Doing.

You

From a very early age, in schools across the world, we learn of humanity's gruesome past. We learn about men killing men; about the wars, genocides and holocausts we have been capable of as civilisations.
Are you saying that none of what we are thought in the history books has really happened?

The Dreamer

If you look for the proof that can affirm or deny the existence of such happenings, you will find both what you're looking for and its opposite.

What apparently exists in time and history are no more than projections of your own states of being. In other words, to find what you're looking for outside, you have to first create it and live it inside.

To find the facts that either confirm or contest those massacres, you have to create the absurd chemistry inside yourself that will catapult you to the most infernal places on earth.

There is no violence in the world, no crime, poverty or famine. There is no war, revolution, terrorism or genocide. No 'acts of god', or unexplainable disaster; no sickness, ageing or death.

There is only you, prisoner of your own morbid fantasies; only you—unconscious victim of the hell you carry inside.

Only you—a forgetful God, who has forgotten his real nature...and has ceased to love himself inside.

You

How is it that a humanity that can think about the complexities of sub-atomic space, look back in deep time to the possible origins of the universe, understand the processes underlying life itself, live beneath the seas, travel at supersonic speed, stand on the moon and create anything it desires, is not able to ensure the happiness of every one of its members?

The Dreamer

As long as you believe that the root of all problems is outside yourself and not within your very being, the crises, the wars, the degradation and unhappiness that you see around you will only perpetuate and worsen.

The world is as you dream it. The world is just reflecting your catastrophic vision of life. Change it and reality will follow. Remember! You yourself are the only one who can save the world.

You are the one who moves the threads of the world.

You've lived a whole life with the description of being menaced by a world that wants to take everything from you, especially what you believe to own.

The goal, the target is always the same—changing the world, changing what you don't like. After having tried with every technique, only dissatisfaction remains, because it's impossible to change the world outside.

Sometimes you'll find yourself in a state that you don't even know where it comes from, a state of powerlessness and you repeat to yourself, it's me, it's me generating all this but you don't know how to change it. The true changing happens through the attention towards this state of powerlessness. Being aware of having limits is a good thing because limits show the way, signal the visible path. People praying, meditating for long hours in an attempt to avoid the pain by renouncing the world will never change an atom of their reality. They will find their efforts to be completely useless.

Instead of running away from it, you need to get closer to this unhappiness, to this state of nausea and death. Don't try to avoid unhappiness when it comes. Are you unhappy? Well, try to be even unhappy! You need to be willing and strongly determined to throw yourself into the abyss of the unknown, in the mouth of evil. Without blaming the others, touch this physical pain that you wrongly believe is caused from something external. Touch it, and you will realise that that pain comes only from within, that it has always been there, there where you have never dared to adventure, where the nausea, the disgust and the fear reside.

What a revolution touching unhappiness! How determined are you to touch this pain? Get rid of everything and dive into pain. You'll figure out that there's nothing, it's only a shadow, a pale and far description that governs and has governed all your life. It's a big lie that pens the doors of paradise. And now the world is at your service, friendship, love, beauty, richness, everyone and everything works for you. Everything.

This technique on the surface may appear as an easy thing to do, but remember this: in the hard moments, it is nearly impossible. When the times get tough, and everything seems to want to crush you, problems get bigger and perpetuate, and you just want to run when the opportunity is there, feel even more the pain, instead of running away from it! When you are in a state of blessing, you'll look for the pain inside of you and you'll never find it anymore. The awareness is light; it's like looking for shadow with a torch. If you carry light in the darkness, it is not dark anymore.

This willingness to meet with the darkness, with the ghosts and with the pain makes you rich. You feel sick?... Perfect! See if you can feel even worse and be even more in pain!

When you are aware of the pain, whether it be physical, emotional or psychological, then you are in charge and no negative event or circumstance can materialise as a reflection of that pain.

If you are not aware, then it will be the pain itself that will take over and you will become a victim of circumstances that you yourself have put in place through your carelessness.

Freedom or Oblivion

Do not fight against any creed or religion.
Do not fight against any form of government.
Do not fight against any nation or civilisation.
You have to fight your inner division, hypocrisy, ignorance and death.

Do not lay the blame on anyone outside, but lay the blame on yourself. You will find that is always true. The secret of all secrets in life is to have no fear. Fearlessness, patience and indomitable will, will make you free. The choice is imperative:

Freedom or oblivion.

There is a way by which fear, disease, poverty aging and death can be slain forever.

There is a way by which victory, prosperity, harmony and happiness can be conquered forever.

There is a way...and the way is the conscious transformation of your inner suffering.

Chapter V
The Others

The others are not aliens.
They are you projected into the world of events. So don't criticise, don't complain or blame the others for their errors because they are only reflecting your own image and will.

Don't try to teach anything to others because they already know all that you want them to know.
Don't try to help or save anybody because there is nobody to help or save but yourself. They perceive all that you perceive. They 'dream' all that you 'dream'. They 'do' all that you 'do'. They harm or love each other in the same measure you harm or love yourself.

Be alert all the time! If you get dreary frozen inside, you will lower the intelligence of the entire world and the others will appear like aliens trying to attack or destroy you.
Remember! The others 'are' your light. The others are your reflection.

The others are the most earnest, sincere thing you possess.
The others exist to tell you what is missing in you.
The others serve and love you with all their strength if you know how to serve and love yourself within.

The others are you, *they are your being materialised, a world of shadow where things happen only because you are.*

*When you see faults in no one other than yourself,
you start to grow.*

*When there are no 'others' to blame but yourself,
you start to own.*

When you realise that there is no one to fight but yourself, you start to win.

The others are the materialisation of your inner states, of your doubts, of your uncertainties.

You have to get sick to meet the crowd just as you now see it. You have to disintegrate to create the others just as they now appear to you.

In the state that you are in, others are pain, fear; the others are suffering. But the others are nothing more than the fruit of your fragmentation, even though this, you can neither see nor understand. The others are you! You think they are something separate from you but you're wrong. They correspond you! Recognise your horror. Each one of them represents a lie, a fear, a mask that you have to leave behind if you want to enter a higher state of existence.

There is no greater adventure, no work more useful than that to encounter others and recognise them as projections of ourselves, of our states, our values.

For many years, for as long as it takes to heal ourselves, encountering others will mean encountering our own sickness, our own failings and our own deaths. For years and years, the world may appear like hell on earth before you recognise that you yourself are the creator of all these shadows that grope around in the world of superstition.

Remember! The others are you in time, and you are the others in absence of time.

Whomever you meet, you are measuring the distance that you have inside from yourself. The other is you in a state of *distance* from yourself, you in time. So go out on a mission to measure this distance. Go through superstition to conquer superstition, go into the world of impressions in order to climb back up to the source, to the real cause. It's a mission to heal yourself. Go out to encounter yourself, to see yourself, to know yourself.

Meeting others is your greatest chance to meet your own hell, to resolve it, to heal it.

Therefore, when you encounter others, go inside yourself and discover what is corresponding with it within you. This way you will know how to 'utilise' that encounter, how to transform it into a step on which you can rest your feet and move on further. You will know how to get rid of the ballast that is holding you prisoner in the sea of superstition.

You will know how to win every battle, realising that the only obstacle is yourself and that the external world is only a reflection of an internal ocean you carry within.

Because of this, when you meet others, feel nothing but gratitude.

When you encounter violent people, be grateful as you may through them recognise and resolve your own violence, when you encounter the poor, be grateful as through them you may transform your own poverty and when you meet the sick through such an encounter, you can heal all the illnesses within you that you still fail to recognise.

So do not blame, criticise or condemn the people who fall in error or fail, but be thankful to them, because they will allow you to recognise in yourself the very cause of all your failures and errors. In the same way, be secretly thankful to all people you encounter and especially to those who criticise you, accuse you, condemn you and even persecute you; you'll hardly be able to pay back what you owe them.

Remember! The others are you yourself in time, and you are the others in absence of time. So, be all gratitude to them!

'Gratefulness is the real gain'.

Encounter someone. In a few minutes, you can know everything about his/her life; you have already lived that life, known that destiny and that of all others like them. The more you know, the more you are capable of entering into yourself, then the more the world disappears.

It is you who gives significance to events, to people. It is in your power to illuminate them for a second and then to switch them off again. You can speed them up or slow them down at will. *The world is an appendix, a world of shadow where things happen only because you are.*

An incomplete person is always waiting for something to happen. But for something to happen, something must bend, break and fall. *Working on being* may appear boring because it strives towards silence, order, perfection and unity which leads to an absence of events, circumstances, encounters and experiences that gave meaning to a life without meaning.

Should perfection be made accessible to you in an instant and without the necessary preparation, you would be swallowed by the abyss of your own ignorance and fear. Unprepared, perfection will appear to you like a ferocious Hydra, a hundred-headed monster created by your own limits of idleness and boredom.

That is why billions of people like you prefer to be part of the *created*, of a fragmented world made by others and governed by chance; the world of a *creator* is too powerful, too crushing for you to be responsible for.

Do not mix or identify with the crowd, you will get stuck! The more you work on yourself for your integrity, the less you will be influenced by the hypnotising forces of the masses. The crowd is the outer representation of your inner division and sorrow. The more you become integrated within yourself, the less you will participate in gathering and meetings. Thousands and thousands of human beings gathered together into squares, stadiums, clubs or theatres, screaming and shouting at a football game or at a rock concert or at a political demonstration, are the most significant manifestation of your deadly inner multitude whose only mission is to destroy you.

You
The solution that you suggest is the solitude of the hermit, which eliminates all contact with the outside world?

Dreamer
No, this is impossible. It is the outcome of another lie. A man who reaches the state of freedom from identification can live anywhere and do anything.

You
How can I then eliminate the 'others', and their influence from my life?

The Dreamer
You can't. As you are today, if you would take away the others, you would be taking away your very life, to eliminate the others from your life you must first realise that the others are the mechanical resonance of your drowsiness. They are the equilibrium of death you carry within. The others are the reflection of your own forgetfulness.

The more a man forgets, the more he relies on others.

The more you love, the more you remember, the more you get closer to yourself, the more the others disappear.

When You Love, the Others Do Not Exist

You

What is the necessity of an external world, when everything comes from within?

The Dreamer

You meet in life all that you secretly hide to yourself.
When you look at yourself in the mirror of the world, you see what you have to get rid of in you.

The Only True Government
You

You mentioned love and yet you talk about the need to stop believing that others exist outside ourselves. How can this be? I have never been the happiest or more alive as when I'm in love with someone.

The Dreamer

Falling in love with someone is a lie.

You cannot fall in love with anybody that is not yourself. And when this happens, you attribute this state of being to the first person you meet, believing that it is that person's qualities to attract you. This sensation is as marvellous as it is dangerous, because nothing and no one outside yourself can contain this joy that explodes inside you.

It is the desperate attempt to pour an ocean into a drinking glass.

In a short time, you realise that the partner into which you had poured all your love, reveals himself or herself unable to sustain this energy and you wait anxiously for a new explosion which could never come again.

In reality, you can sincerely love somebody only if you first learn how to love yourself.

You

If we were all to do as you say, and seek a life of solitude, who will then govern the political complexities of a country, manage the economic turns of a nation or quell the religious, racial and social discriminations that set the world in turmoil?

The Dreamer

The only true government is self-government.

As long as you believe that politicians have the power to govern your outer life and religions put order in your inner one, you will be strongly disappointed. Then, before the outside world is destroyed by your politicians, priests and scientists, enter into your inner world alone and touch your integrity.

It is the only safety left, the only shelter against any viruses and evil, against any terrorism and nuclear war, against global suicide.

Self-government is the only government that can govern the world. The power of being present inside projects a place where there are no divisions, no conflicts, no boundaries between yourself and the others. Where suffering is, your blindness is its very cause, and where conflicts are, your suffering is their very root,

To have another world, you have to change your dream, and this is the most difficult task.

Your healing will be humanity's healing, and your integrity will be the salvation of the world.

You don't dedicate time to yourself. You are always 'away from home', away from yourself, from your true nature of creator.

You do not dream! Well-being to you is being with other people, in the midst of people and in their shadow. Being in the outside world for you is as necessary, as indispensable, as breathing. For you to spend time alone is unbearable. You search for the certainty of the outside world; you try to find it in the eyes of others. This is because you do not love yourself.

This inability to love yourself leads to a kind of internal self-destruction that may materialise in various guises, through self-harm, drugs, alcohol, harmful attitudes and habits, provoking apparently unpredictable and involuntary accidents. The incapacity to be alone, the need for others, to lie and to hide, are the unconscious symptoms of a self-destructive inclination.

Solitude is fortitude. Solitude has to be a friend. You need to learn how to feel good on your own, loving yourself. To stay by yourself means to build yourself, to strengthen yourself. It is necessary to know how to transform loneliness into solitude.

If you do not live beautiful moments in a conscious, intentional, creative solitude, life will force you to live bad moments in a forced loneliness.

Close your eyes and feel your own company. This way, by being with yourself, you acquire power. Power cannot be given to you by others. Power is self-mastery.

Build yourself from the inside. Become your own teacher.

Power is the elimination of everything you were taught in your first education. Power is the elimination of everything you believe you have understood, from false certainty, from second-hand knowledge and thoughts.

The others are the projections of your shadows. They are your inner states in action. When certain states disappear, corresponding events and people also disappear. To go towards light means to leave the shadows behind. To ascend, to integrate yourself and to illuminate yourself, you must sacrifice something. The life of a Dreamer will not accept even a single atom of uncertainty. Understand this and you will either give yourself up to sleep, to justifying, to complaining and accusing, or you will dedicate yourself to your evolution, to your improvement.

The others are there only if you get further away from yourself, only if you deteriorate and disintegrate into a million pieces. People go out, go to restaurants, to the cinema, to a club, takes part in social gatherings to be with others, to encounter others.

But when the others have too much significance in your life, sooner or later you will be trapped. If you rely solely on external events, if you wait for others, searching for approval or validation in their eyes or if you rely on sex, on food, on sleep as the only means to *'feel alive'*, you will become small like a grain of sand.

Rely on yourself! Realise that you have all the power inside yourself and you will *be*. Liberate yourself from time. Liberate yourself from the world, from the creation that gave birth to you. The attachments making you feel secure: a career, a marriage a child, a role, are putting an internal fence around a little piece of existence, circumscribing it, limiting you and making you feel secure.

As of today, the events, the happenings and the others make you feel alive. You mistake experiences for life but nothing can ever come from the external world. There is no experience and knowledge that you can learn or take from the others.

The others are your illusory conviction that something exists outside yourself that can take care of you, divert you, enthuse you or hurt you. The need for others means the need for this illusion and the need for something that doesn't exist.

But the others are a trap that you have created. This illusion will always make you poorer, fragment you into a thousand pieces and completely disintegrate you; it will make you get older, will sicken you and ultimately kill you.

Only the awareness that the others are your mirror, the manifestation of what you are, makes you belong to a higher level of intelligence.

When you meet someone, you have to use them as luminous steps; you have to know in a fleeting moment to which category and typology of people they belong, swallow their entire existence and go beyond. The others are there only for your understanding, to reveal your inner states and take you further. Any person you meet and any situation or role you find yourself in, must be used like a dress that you wear and change when it no longer fits you.

This is the game of encounters.

For a long time, you will continue to meet the same characters but at a higher level of responsibility until you realise that there is nobody to know, to meet or use 'out there', but yourself.

With this comprehension, the world gets back into the right proportion and becomes very small. You realise that it is fragile, that it needs nourishment and that it needs to be given life, and only you can do that.

You are the Dreamer that creates the others, creates the events, creates and knows to be the sole maker of every atom of the universe. So, stop. Close your eyes and enter into a state of deathlessness. Fill yourself up with life and then meet the world, the others, the events and realise that all that you encounter in the world of events, all the experiences that you may live are just a reflection of something you have already conquered within.

Loneliness and fear can only be won through self-awareness.

You search for other people to fill your solitude, without understanding that solitude is the reason and the principle source of your richness.

Spend more time being in your own company, free from any kind of conditioning, do it intentionally if you wish to achieve a life rich in all senses. The multiplicity of events, circumstances, facts, insignificant experiences and the others, in our lives match our incapability of living in solitude.

The more we live in solitude, the more events disappear, to make space for those more intense and more real.

Loneliness is the price and solitude is the prize.

You have to constantly abandon all that which you've experienced because experiences are time, and whatever is in time or ruled by time is false.

*Shed your experiences like a
snake changing its skin.*

One day, you will understand that what you call experience is not an external phenomenon but something that happens within yourself and that only through your creative imagination believe to be external and real. In reality, whatever you experience, it lasts only but a moment and disappears in the blink of an eye.

The Bible says: "Lot's wife disobeyed God's warning by 'looking back' and watching the destruction of Sodom and Gomorrah. She was punished by being turned into a 'pillar of salt'."

How many little pillars of salt lie in your own time-body—in your own imaginary living past? And how many pillars of salt you will still encounter in your own being and in life, walking the streets daily, before you can realise that the past is dust and that nothing has ever happened before this very now?

You can't look back!

You can't recapture anything from the past because there is no past—nothing existed before this very moment. Everything appears as a new experience moment by moment and disappears instantly leaving the sensation that something really happened.

You
What about helping others? The ones that are less fortunate, less able; the ones who live a life of hardship by no faults of their own. Shall we just ignore people who are in need?

The Dreamer
Respect anybody for the role they naturally play in life, and never try to change their horrors and fears in something that they could never contain, sustain or be responsible for.

Then don't talk of helping another, focus instead on the only thing you can do; getting rid of your own need of help

Remember! You can only give what you are.
Accidents Are Never Accidental

You

And the people who find themselves victims of random acts of violence, who are caught in a car accident over which they have no control, who are attacked or robbed when walking in the street?

The Dreamer

Everyone encounters only oneself. The others, the world, the experiences, the facts, the phenomena, are only the deferments.

The more you are separated from yourself, the more space must be filled with others, with events, with experiences, nice or nasty as they may be.

You have to learn to go back to yourself, to the cause. You carry a grimace inside you at all times, a tight pain, a pain that you have no clue is even there. Have a good look at it. It is death.

You have to learn to recognise and cure this wound, this inner death; if it remains unchecked, it will continue to attract illnesses, conflicts and accidents in your life. As soon as you feel that pain and that anguish, you should exclaim, "Hey you! What are you doing here? I am the head of the household. Nobody gets an atom in here without my permission!"

Remember! Accidents are never accidental, but the impeccable planning of an unconscious will.

Each man lives what he projects. No one finds himself in any situation he did not, consciously or unconsciously, ask for.

The world you live in is the world you dream of.

You

What should we do then when the world outside gets tough or threatening?

The Dreamer

Let's start with what you shouldn't do:
You must not react, not react as you always do to everything. If you find the strength to not react to the outer circumstances, you will no longer be at the mercy of life. So, do not identify with the difficulties and unhappiness of the outer world. Isolate yourself internally from life and don't let its events crush you.

No one and nothing can hurt you or even touch you if you neither identify nor react to the external events.

Non-identifying means not getting lost or drowned in your own image reflected in the troubled waters of the world.

Remember! There is nothing to fear in darkness. Confusion, uncertainty, anger, despair and pain.

All the attacks, conditionings, injustice, chaos and crisis coming from the outer world, are all excellent conditions for your growth.

You

So, we should never take any action?

The Dreamer

Do not dare to change the world outside, you will fail. The world is only the cinematographic representation of your own being.

Could you ever imagine getting something real by scratching a movie-screen? Anything coming from the world, from 'out there', can only help you to recognise in yourself the true source of all your troubles, limitations and misery. Therefore, do not take any action; let all outer events, circumstances, experiences and relations with the others, fall into that place within yourself where integrity reigns supreme and where all waste, trash and ballast will be transformed into a new substance, new energy, new life.

There is nothing outside of you that is before you.

The Individual and the Mass

Individual comes from indivisible.

Individual identifies a man who has achieved a state of inner integrity, of oneness, of love.

The common man, who we can call '*dividual*', is a *mass*, a legion divided among one thousand 'I' eternally fighting against each other, torn by conflicting thoughts and emotions, divided from himself and from others, without identity, without ideas, without love.

Man is not a unity as he is supposed to be, but a multitude. To be a multitude means to be trapped in an unreal, unescapable, self-created system of false beliefs and lies.

In man, there is both the project to become a mass and that to become an individual, to reluctantly take the road towards the insect or to rediscover his origins of god.

But wherever an individual is born immediately the mass, the antagonist force rises up, a crowd ready to eliminate him.

The mass is the antagonist of the individual. It has always been, without exceptions, at all latitudes and throughout time; the struggle between the individual and the mass, the persecution of individuality, has been a permanent feature in human history.

We need the individual and at the same time, as species, we have an irrepressible instinct of supressing him.

The individual scares us, the extent of his ideas, the width of his breath, the scope of his dream, his aliveness and incorruptibility, cause us unbearable pain. Only being in his presence, listening to his voice, or watching him act, puts us in front of our laziness, our ugliness, our unbearable deformity. Too much effort is required to change. We cannot stand the comparison. We need to destroy him, to suppress that voice that tirelessly pushes towards inner unity, towards improvement, towards integrity.

And yet, nothing is created without being first dreamed by the individual.

Behind all that we can see, perceive, touch and feel, behind all material and immaterial conquest of our civilisation, there is always a special man with his dream.

Only an individual can dream.

Only the individual is creative and only thanks to individuals, we achieve material and moral progress, the inheritance of art, values, brilliant and noble ideas that still nourish our civilisation.

Let's change the dreamed. Let's change the mirrored.
Let's change the events, the others, the world.
Let's change the past. Let's change destiny.

*Let's change the impossible,
the invincible, the inevitable.*

Let's change the very cause of all troubles and difficulties: the unchangeable You.

Learn to stay by yourself or you will suffer a lot.

At whatever stage of his life, if a man could observe what really happens within himself, he will see that he is living in a state of unhappiness, of discontent.

To be alive, you must train. This training is *a full-time commitment*. Learn to feel good alone!

If you don't train yourself, you will strive to stay amongst people, you will seek a job you don't like and will find yourself in a marriage that doesn't make you happy, all just to be with others.

Learn to stay well on your own. The world should be constructed inside yourself by you and yourself only. *Inside and outside don't exist.* Only creativity exists. In the crowd, you give up being a creator and are prone to be created. To live forever, you must not miss a second; one second of forgetting will make you fall into the inferno and lose all you have gained in years of work.

What I am telling you is about living permanently in a state of victory.

Happiness and success can't be lived on the outside, with the others. They can only be created inside and in this very moment.

What you see outside has already happened.

You
Is your world full of people, events and experiences as is mine?

The Dreamer
No, it is full of myself. In my world, everything falls in the right place and nothing ever goes wrong.

You

Don't you ever feel lonely or sad to be permanently, or most of the time, by yourself; separated for so long from the others and from the rest of the world?

The Dreamer

The absolute, the totality to be such can never feel lonely and neither feel sad or tired.

The totality of your being contains, sustains and nourishes the entire universe. How could the universe then feel miserable, lonely or, as someone has dreary imagined, come to an end, if you, the dreamer, creator and sustainer of its very existence is permanently dreaming of it?

Train to have paradise inside: *a portable Paradise.*
There is no role, friend, relationship, that can make us stay in paradise, only ourselves. No marriage, music, sex, drugs and no priest, master or guru can carry us to paradise, only ourselves.

Remember! Two worlds don't exist, you and the others.

The more you are, the less the others are. The more you are close to yourself, the more you are in touch with the '*here and now*', and the less the external world with its apparent game of opposites will be attractive to you.

Once this is understood, all the superfluities will go away. Everything will become more profound.

The more you get closer to yourself, the less space there is for hate and the more there is for life to become deeper, to become higher.

Your life is not made of outer events but of inner states. So, stop looking elsewhere. Know yourself! Be yourself!

Return to the source, dive deep within and, whatever happens in the world, be 'inaccessible'. When you are free of the world, you can do something about it. As long as you are identified with it, lost in it, prisoner of it, you are helpless to change it, and whatever you do, on the contrary, will aggravate its conditions.

Once you realise that all comes from within, that the world in which you live has not been projected onto you but by you, your fear comes to an end.

Remain in a state of inner attention and fearlessness no matter what you may face in life, whether you have profit or loss, pleasure or pain, sickness or health, victory or defeat, whether people praise or criticise you. Remain in a state of inner harmony and silence regardless of what is going on outside yourself.

This is the way you can change the world.

Remember! There is no violence in the world, no crime, poverty or famine. There is no war, revolution, terrorism or genocide, no 'acts of god', or unexplainable disaster, no sickness, ageing or death. There is only you, prisoner of your own morbid fantasies, only you, unconscious victim of the hell you carry inside. Only you, a forgetful God, who has forgotten his real nature and never loved himself inside.

Are you a creator or a victim of the world? Are you a hunter or the hunted? Are you dreaming the world or dreamt by it? This depends upon your level of understanding.

There is nothing more objective than subjectivity. And there is nothing more subjective than objectivity. Vision and reality are one and the same thing. In this precise instant, you create the world that you inhabit. If you believe in separation and in the struggle for survival, then you'll see your inner fragmentation and pain reflected all around and your perceptions governed by doubt and fear. You will dwell in a world of death and of bodies fighting, killing and devouring each other.

Believing to see makes you the creator and master of the whole world. Seeing to believe makes you slave and victim of a painful reality that you, yourself project.

Remember, this in your own life when it seems that nothing is going right and when you feel you are mistaking something. You don't make mistakes! You can only do what you are. A machine doesn't make errors. It does just what it is programmed to do. It cannot change its own design, its own nature or its own destiny. Machines are born and die as machines. They cannot come out of their mechanical order. No matter how hard they try, they remain a puppet, moved by external forces.

Life is what you dream it to be.

If you listen to yourself, if you record what you feel and what seems to be happening inside of you in just this moment, you will realise that it is instead what happens throughout the whole day, every day of your existence.

Identified as you are with the world, with superficiality and all that keeps you strenuously occupied every day, you can't realise that these states of being that you rarely are able to see within yourself govern your life. They loom over you, oppress you and subject you to thousands of inner deaths every day until bringing you to final physical death.

Ordinary man is condemned to death.

The best indicator of your level of understanding is how you deal with life's challenges and attacks when they come. You can use life's challenges to awaken you, or you can let them pull you into even deeper sleep.

It is impossible to find yourself in a war if you don't produce death within yourself or if you don't dream of it. War, poverty, failure, disease, death or any other disaster are not objective realities. They are not outside yourself. They become real only if you dream of them.

But you are so strongly convinced that the universe is a hostile place where you are victim of forces outside, over which you have no control at all. You have taken your internal divisions and distortions as something brought about by the world outside when, in reality, they are merely projected out into the screen of external reality from your inner, fragmented being.

In order to fill the gap between dream and reality you have to first get rid of your belief in illusions, you have to realise that your beliefs in separation, limitation, lack, loss, pain, struggle, sickness, birth and death are not real but only a description of reality.

You have to learn how not to lie, first of all to yourself. It's time to abandon your conflictual vision of the world.

It's time for you to die to all which is lifeless.

It's time to be reborn. It is the greatest adventure a man can possibly imagine: the regaining of his own lost integrity.

You

When I look back at some of the most painful moments of my life, I am often overwhelmed with feelings of regret.
Can we ever learn to heal the wounds of our past?

The Dreamer

You cannot change the past if you don't understand that it is this present which gives form to the past.

Whatever you attain in this instant is simultaneously transferred in all directions. If the present is made perfect, everything in your past will be aligned with this perfection.

Each event of the past is just a resonance of the vibrations that your body is sending right now.

You
But how I could I possibly change the past if it has already happened?

Dreamer
Raise your now, and your stiff, weary, decrepit memory will disappear, and a luminous, vibrant, new past will beckon you. The higher your now, the greater will be your history and the more magnificent your destiny.

As long as you believe in an external world, then make use of it. Let all the experiences, events and circumstances fall in a place within yourself where you can filter the most useful and eliminate what is useless.

The others, the world—this is the place where all your useless material can be transformed in energy and brand-new life. What you see and encounter outside is only a faded shadow of your inner space, a pale manifestation of your inner responsibility.

Look at and see humanity surrounding you like puppets, you attended their schools and went through the same books, all of which only served to make you unhappier, deadlier.

You have to learn how to be free from the identification with the world. Ignore everything that comes from the outside. The more you are whole, the greater and more harmonious your life. To take from the outside, as the fruit of the forbidden tree, is to forget that integrity, is to lose *heaven*.

Focus your attention inside yourself and force yourself to be happy just as you unconsciously force yourself to be miserable and full of troubles and mishaps. Remember! All comes from within, and therefore no accidents, no betrayals, evils, threats or dangers can happen to a man who is simply aware of himself.

Force yourself to be happy, just as you unconsciously force yourself to be 'unhappy' and full of troubles and accidents. Accidents cannot happen to a man who is aware of himself inside.

When attacks and malice arrive, don't accuse the world, the others or the circumstances. Take time, at least a little time, a few seconds, to listen to yourself inside. Something's bothering you, threatening you… Chase your shadows inside, like you would do with an intruder, hunt like prey your falsity and doubts—the beast within you that devours you.

It is your blind belief in the external that kills you. You find your real self only when you have reached a state of total ignorance from the outside.

When you are no longer lured and cured by the outside world, your reality will reflect the harmony, the beauty and the wealth that you have gained within you.

You have to see the whole movement of life, apparently obscure and conflictual, as a marvellous single, unitary process. Religions, ideologies, sciences, arts, businesses, all the revolutions, wars, terrorism and crime, the endless human divisions, disorders and sorrow, seen from above are the various expressions of a single movement dictated by your inner unity. Seen from below, they appear as the atrocious and painful reflex images of your fragmented being.

It all depends upon you! When your vision brightens and intensifies, your outer reality can only express the same thing.

Light, order, beauty and perfection are the inevitable creation of a world seen from above.

Wings glued on with the glue of accusation and self-justification will fall away, and only the one who has constructed 'real wings' can face the great adventure.

The one who wins his internal conflicts will win also the external ones.

The one who unites within will unite without.

The one who overcomes his inner limits, will liberate the world from all boundaries.

You

As I look at you, you seem to be sure of yourself and safe, without limits and without problems. How is it that your experience is so different from ours?

The Dreamer

You can see the world only through the idea you have of yourself.

It's your inner attitude that differs and not the outer experience. As you think yourself to be, so the world appears to you. The difference lies in you alone.

Know yourself as a whole, and you will see the world as it is—a single, indivisible, complete and harmonious unity.

You

But if by applying your principles, you have succeeded in changing yourself and, with you, the entire universe. How do you explain then, that in spite of your efforts, the world still remains the same as before?

The Dreamer

The world is such because you are such and nothing can change it if you don't change. It is 'your own world' which remains the same, and not mine.

You have to realise that there has been no other world before than that one you're dreaming right now.

You

What obstructs the knowledge of the Dreamer from being recognised throughout the world?

The Dreamer

It's you. It's your own limitation. The moment you accept and know that you are the Dreamer, nothing and nobody can in any way hold it back.

Out of the Crowd

If you remain whole, your vanity will disappear, and with it, the absurd theatre of appearances.
If you remain intact, time will vanish and with it, all that is not real: 'suffering' for example.
If you remain untouched, you'll see the world in its absolute perfection and the others as they really are: gods, omnipotent and immortal as yourself.

The world is our masterpiece.
For better and for worse, in success and in failure, in death and in eternity, in joy and in pain, in doubt and in certainty, in abundance and in privation, in scarcity and in riches.

The world, this personal universe, is always our own masterpiece. We are its artists and its creators even when we have forgotten to be so.

Remember,
life will test you until you either give up or go beyond.

Chapter VI
Being and Having

You can only have what you are responsible for.

*Financial power, like love, obeys the same principle.
Your wealth corresponds exactly to the prosperity you are able to produce within yourself.*

Inner responsibility and absence of fear eliminate all limits, and are therefore the very source of every fortune and riches.

*Money like love is an inner matter.
Money is a state of being.
Money-affluence manifests in time what
you have conquered through inner responsibility
and creative victory, which is love.*

All comes from within.
    Even money comes from inside; it is produced within. How?
    By eliminating the illusion of not having any.
    Being and having are one and the same.
    A man's richness, welfare and standard of living, as well as a nation's or an entire society's, do not depend on the availability and abundance of means and material resources, but on the amplitude of their being—in the same way, the way we feel, think, act, our aspirations and the profundity of our ideas, what we believe in and the scope of our dream are what determines our destiny.
    There is nothing outside of yourself for which you are not the cause.

Having depends on being just like a shadow depends for its dimension and form on the object that is projecting it.

    This truth has always eluded the ordinary mankind's comprehension, for being exists in absence of time and having taken place in space and time.
    What prevents us from seeing the perfect balance existing between being and having is this very time-factor that, like a smokescreen, deceptively separates them just by illusion. Sublimed having becomes being and materialised being becomes having—however, time pulls a physiological curtain over the eyes of men and makes them blind to this truth.
    In some cases, if momentarily favoured by an event or by external circumstances. Having can appear to be superior to being for a *period of time*; and this is sufficient enough to convince you that being and having are completely separate and independent realities from each other.
    But if, by magic, you could succeed in compressing time, the years of a man's life, or the centuries of a civilisation's cycle, you would see the perfect correspondence between having and being—you would understand that in a timeless vision, they are the same, identical realities on different levels.

'The greatest misfortune a man can encounter is having without being.
Should great wealth be given to you by mere chance, it will certainly also be taken away from you in the same way.
Real lasting success can only be achieved when you have first lived, experienced and conquered success within'.

    Being is not in opposition to having, it lives on a higher level. Being and having are the same reality vibrating at different speeds and occupying different steps on the scale of existence. If you were able to emerge from your time-bound universe and rise along a timeless vertical, you could see that having is not independent from being but is its projection.

If you were to raise your vision, free yourself from the chains of time and space, having and being, economics and ethics, vision and reality would become one. Contrarily, if you were to lower your vision, you would enter in a world of multiplicity, of division and see only reality in its apparent nature of struggle and conflict, of disorder and injustice, a universe governed only by 'chance'.

You can have only what you are.
The more you are, the more you have.
The more you have, the more you have to be.

The acknowledgement that 'having is being' removes one of the oldest prejudices of man and revolutionises his conceptual schemes. It is not the having that allows us to do and to be, but the being that allows us to do and consequently to have. Going over this form of mass hypnosis means leaving a flat vision of the world behind us and entering a *vertical vision* where there are layers of reality corresponding to endless levels of being.

'Having is being' is the key to understanding the most complex and vital questions regarding men's lives, the roles and places they occupy and the diversity of their destinies. The history of mankind is an unceasing pursuit of doing and having more; the progress of the civilisation coincides with the development of greater abilities to produce, transform, communicate, travel, as well as destroy, guided by the greed for possession, by predatory instincts never appeased—the echo of an animal longing.

The invisible dimension of ideas, the world of causes, runs vertically to history and destiny. Every conquest in the visible, every development in the capability of accomplishing and having has always been anticipated by a gain in the being. Scientific knowledge and technological progress proceed at the same rate with the knowledge that man has of himself and the level of integrity reached

A man, a civilisation, a country, have the ability to do and to own only what they have already achieved in their being; events and circumstances in their history and all they meet, whether good or bad, has a perfect correspondence to their level of being, to the breadth of their ideas, to the depth of their values.

In nature, as well as in economics, every recovery proceeds from the inside to the outside, from the invisible to the visible, from being to having.

There will come a time when all writings, music, compositions and all scientific and technological discoveries will not belong any more to their creator, author or inventor, but to the whole of humanity who has the inalienable right to reproduce and distribute them in every way possible and for every imaginable use. And no one will be accused of stealing, plagiarism or theft of intellectual property because the new humanity will not believe that the universe of creation is subject to attribution, or that anyone can claim rights over the universal power of creation.

You

'Work hard, and you will be successful' was my grandfather's childhood advice to me. And so, I did: I worked three jobs to pay for college, and never stopped working since.

And yet, after many years, my life is not what I imagined it to be. I had to abandon all my desires and ambitions to settle for a job I don't like.

Why is it so? Isn't hard work enough to make it in this life?

The Dreamer

In the world of integrity, being, knowing, doing and having happen simultaneously; they are one and the same thing.

In your world, you attempt to live your life backwardly. That is, having for doing, doing for knowing and knowing for being, when the way it actually works is the reverse. You can 'possess' only what 'you are' responsible for, then being for knowing, knowing for doing and finally doing for having.

Remember! Do not desire, deserve.

You

It seems that wherever you go in the world, the most common concern within any business, family or individual is the lack of money. I too, very often, find myself worrying about my financial situation. What can we do about it?

The Dreamer

Money is only a by-product. You will find all the resources you need if you don't let the outer world take over.

Just go back to the dream and win the battle, which is only with yourself. Let wealth-consciousness take place within you and all the financial problems will instantly disappear.

It is not the lack of money that determines your limits and constrictions. But vice versa, it is your inner limits and misery that determine your lack of resources and financial misfortune.

For a man of integrity, the new man, doing precedes thinking or planning, the solution precedes the problem and victory precedes the battle, so that the latter disappears.

When you find yourself facing a financial problem, don't be discouraged. Make yourself still. Straighten up your backbone. Breathe deeply.

Turn all your attention toward your inner being. Take command of your wavering, quivering feelings and then affirm what you most want to achieve with steadfast determination and certainty. This will bring infinite resources to your business and justice to your life.

The closer you are to the 'dreamer in you', the less room you have for fear, doubt and failure.

You

But how can I live a happier, wealthier life, when everything and everyone seem to conspire against me?

The Dreamer

You are the richest and most powerful being on Earth...but you don't know it. This 'not knowing' makes you miserable, unhappy...and mortal. You're the freest being in the universe...but you don't know it. This makes you the most fragile creature on Earth.

Your level of freedom and happiness, and your wealth as well, depend on your level of consciousness and integrity and yet your whole life is dedicated to demonstrate to yourself the opposite—that everything is an effect of the world, that fault lies on outer circumstances.

Living in luxury is a state of being that needs to be created from within. Be a king and the kingdom will come!

The banks you see outside are only a pale reflection of the resources you have within you. Its vaults are inside you and can be opened on command. 'Money is an inner matter'.

So, don't worry about money. Worry about yourself, about your integrity. When money is needed, it will be right there. Trust yourself, trust your dream and you will have all the money necessary to match a beautiful life.

'If you bet on yourself, life will bet on you'.

Everyone wants to make money but few succeed. And yet, making money is easy. True wealth is already inside you, you only have to liberate it of the ballast and bring it out.

Remember! If you have nothing that at present satisfies you, the fault is only within. You will never get what you want as long as your being remains as it is. You have to change yourself to get new understanding, new meaning, new life and consequently attract events of a higher order.

Changing yourself means, first of all, 'getting rid of yourself'. In order to be born 'at a higher level', you have to die 'at a lower one'.

The wealth of a man, the success of an enterprise, the financial destiny of a nation are no more than a reflection of their philosophy, the materialisation of the ways of thinking, the system of values and beliefs of that man, of that company, of that nation.

In the near future, every organisation from the smallest to the largest multinational company will be ideological. This will determine its success, its longevity.

Organisations of the future will need people with a much higher level of responsibility that today's employees can offer. The rational, provincial, nineteenth-century capitalism that dominated the economy for more than two hundred years, is turning in front of our eyes into an intuitive, emotional, creative capitalism of worldwide dimensions.

Employment is a modern form of slavery; to be an employee is not a social status, a role in an organisation or the effect of a contract. To be an employee is the effect of a condition of being.

People motivated by money are limited. Only people guided by their dream, led by their inner intuition will be able to project at will a world of abundance and fortunes. They do what they love and not what makes money.

Remember. Nothing coming from 'out there' can make you whole, happy or wealthy. Your real personal prosperity can only come from within. Only the 'dream' can make us free, overcome all our limits. Only the 'dream' can transform poverty into prosperity, difficulties into intelligence, fear into love.

You will never climb above a certain level of responsibility or succeed financially, if deep down you associate having money or prosperity to immorality or lack of ethics. A false, negative association will create a war inside you, a sense of guilt, a process of self-sabotage that will wipe out all your ability to succeed not only financially, but in all fields of life.

When you have freed yourself of unhappiness, fear and negative emotions, the world will bring gifts beyond your imagination, surround you with wealth and it will regenerate effortlessly.

You

The world is changing so fast. New technologies and new competitors, which threaten my business, seem to be emerging every day. How can I control what is going around me, and how can I become a successful leader?

The Dreamer

A true leader finds solutions, decides things and overcomes impossible issues, wins battles and conflicts, climbs mountains and crosses oceans through his own inner states, that is, within himself, in solitude, in silence, in stillness.

The people he attracts and works with are the outer expression of his inner responsibility, and it is as faithful and intelligent as his own incorruptible commitment to the dream. He never asks for anything because he knows that no help can come from outside. He knows that within himself, he's got all the capacity and strength to create all the resources he needs.

He knows that the only tool necessary for his victory and success is his own inner integrity.

You

But if understanding, integrity or the totality of being can be reached in an instant, why is it taking me so long?

The Dreamer

Years and layers of neglect, negative emotions and false ideas have kept you in a tattered, powerless state.

You have to understand that even if you could catch a glimpse of your totality, you would not be able to sustain it. You must work hard to uncover and strengthen your will. Your will is for your being like muscles are for your body: the more you dedicate to strengthening it, the more you will be rewarded with glimpses of totality.

Integrity, then, will not be a state you temporarily experience, but your very permanent reality.

Whatever you focus upon, expands.

You believe yourself to be living a life of struggle and financial need because you are unlucky, instead of recognising that your belief system is rooted in scarcity thinking.

If you spend a great deal of your life energy focusing on scarcity, that is what you are going to produce and expand in your life.

So, focus all your attention on prosperity and never allow any thought of narrowness to enter into your life.

On the Edge of the Abyss

Having is being. Being is having.

In order to *have,* you have to first *be*. To access greater wealth, you have to enter into an area of superior being.

You have to stop, observe yourself, understand; you need to breathe in and go beyond. To go beyond means returning to a higher state that watches from above a humanity that identifies with the external reality that flounders in a sea of fear. It's a state of timelessness, a vertical time, where wealth can neither degrade nor be stolen.

Remember! To go beyond, a man will have to confront everything that his incomprehension, his lack of will and his lack of integrity have created over years and layers of forgetfulness.

He will be attacked by everything and everyone, abandoned by everything and everyone, tested until he either gives up or goes beyond like the ancient tale of the monk and the tiger:

'A monk, while out walking one day, is confronted by a ferocious, man-eating tiger. He slowly backs away from the animal, only to find that he is trapped at the edge of a high cliff; the tiger snarls with hunger, and pursues the monk. His only hope of escape is to suspend himself over the abyss by holding onto a vine that grows at its edge.

As the monk dangles from the cliff, he looks down to the bottom of the abyss and sees a second tiger leaping powerfully to paw the air just beneath him. He tightens his grip just as two mice—one white and one black—begin to gnaw on the vine he is clutching on.

If he climbs back up, the tiger will surely devour him; if he stays, then there is the certain death of a long fall onto the jagged rocks. The slender vine begins to give way, and death is imminent...'

—From the *Ancient Zen Story by the Buddha*

What is the solution?

The solution is to wake up! But what does 'wake up' mean? When life attacks you, when you are threatened by evil, when your debts so heavily outweigh your credits and difficulties seem insurmountable, when you are trapped in a corner and you can't see any escape route, how can you wake up?

A man should be grateful for always being in this position: on the edge of the abyss. What you call adversity, arrives to facilitate your passage. If you don't have something inside yourself that aims high above your ordinary states of being, it is easy to give up and to fall.

Once you know the way up, everything comes back to you, and a higher level of wealth and existence is created in every sense.

But an ordinary man does not have the capacity to rise up and to stand. He reacts, gives in to the attack, avoids responsibility and enters into the lowest circles of the Inferno. Sooner or later, everyone finds themselves suspended above the abyss, clinging to a root that is about to give way, with their back to the wall and no apparent way out. That is when the gateway to access a higher zone of existence is opened. You cannot stop. Indulging leads you to catastrophe. What you have, you own only if you transcend it.

If you don't dare, even what you believe you own will attack you. If you do not enter into a state of fearlessness, whatever you possess will get smaller and smaller until it vanishes.

'Evil is yesterday's good that you have failed to transcend and raise to a higher order'.

It is not about any technique or managerial strategy. It is about inner capacity. Every day requires the effort to access new levels, to reach new heights.

Once you get rid of all the limits and boundaries you carry inside, you will see that everything is perfect, that all the attacks that arrive are blessings in disguise, and all difficulties that you find on your way are but the stepping stones to perfection. They arrive because something inside you is asking, is aspiring to a greater wealth.

In a state of fearlessness, nothing is impossible to either overcome or to achieve.

The moment you dream a new dream, you are creating also the antagonist that will help you to realise it, an antagonist of equal strength that can make the path towards its realisation visible and possible,

When this occurs, when the antagonist appears, how difficult and how courageous you must be to not cry out for help, how much faith in oneself and how much certainty to put one foot in the abyss and know that the entire universe will sustain you! Try to observe when you are at the mercy of your emotions and how easily you can be devastated, depressed or angered by its actions. You have to create in yourself enough trust and safety to fully experience the world and its apparent evil and injustice instead of being paralysed by it or falling into it.

Remember! The antagonist, the enemy, is a special propellant. The greater our degree of responsibility, the more ruthless the antagonist's attack. The antagonist's one and only aim, concealed by his mercilessness, is your victory. No one on earth can love you more than the antagonist. No one can meet an antagonist greater than himself, or superior to his own intelligence and ability. However horrible, menacing or unbeatable it may appear, the confrontation with the antagonist is always a fair fight and the forces in play are always equivalent.

Only in the absence of time does the antagonist disappear and, with him, every conflict. But how could you live without the antagonist? The antagonist gives you a role, a job and even a name, a family and a purpose in life. Behind his apparent ruthlessness hides your greatest ally, your most faithful servant. The antagonist's sole and unique aim is your victory.

You have made great efforts to climb the mountain of your apparent difficulties to overcome the antagonist only to find that he never really existed if not within you. Your intelligence will grow with his power, your power with his intelligence. Because the antagonist is you!

The more tangible or visible is the antagonist, the more imaginary it is. Any fight or war or enemy can only exist in your imagination. It's your inner conflict which is itself unreal that projects a world of nonsense, a world of shadows that you believe to be real.

Don't forget: the world is the dreamed, and the dreamed can never hurt you. The dreamed is entirely depending on you. You are the sole Dreamer and creator. You are the very cause of its existence. Without you, the world disappears; the world owes you all.

The Will

Will is not a thought, or an object, or a hope, or a wish, or something to attempt.

Will is what makes you succeed when your thoughts tell you that you are defeated and when your feelings tell you that the task you try to undertake is beyond your capacity.

An ordinary man can grasp the things of the world only with his hands or his senses, but a man of integrity uses his will to create and project the world he is dreaming of. An ordinary man perceives the world as a separate reality. A man of integrity knows that the world and his own vision are one and the same thing.

Will is not something that you can develop or achieve, but something that you have hidden and forgotten, something that you already possess and that you are called now to 'remember' and reveal in all its power and beauty.

In passing from one state of being to a higher one, even in the slightest degree, there is a gap, an interval where you are bound to suffer inner stress and doubts.

If you know at the moment how to keep a certain alertness and calm and not let yourself be overcome, you will be brought into a higher level of understanding and overwhelmed by a world of light, certainty, justice, wealth and beauty. When you are fearful, the whole world is overwhelmed by fear and violence, when you are doubtful everything is uncertain. To change your life, you have to change your inner states, not your behaviour—and this is a matter of will.

Will governs your inner being, which is the real world, and has nothing to do with the outer events. When you return to a state of fearlessness and integrity through the power of will, you will find that everything on earth is perfect.

Remember this when you seem to be facing impossible odds, when it seems that everything and everyone is coming against you and you are called to make a decision, to act: you have to stop! The measure of the responsibility of a man is to know when to *stop*.

Real 'doing' is suspending every action until you are fully 'in charge' of yourself. Three seconds are enough to take full possession of yourself. The ability to stop before touching the world, this immobility, creates the force that then will manifest in action.

When you are in that state, you bring awareness, richness, beauty, joy and happiness. It's your responsibility to not give up even an inch of this well-being. Its disappearance means having fallen into the imaginary, into a lie.

The world doesn't need your complaining. Battles are not won spreading one's own fear, accusing, self-justifying or feeling sorry for yourself. The world doesn't even need your help, but it desperately needs to be recreated, to be reinvented! And only you can do it, by taking charge of the totality of your being and commanding three seconds in an absolute inner silence. Three seconds in touch with your very self.

They contain the infinite. It's a powerful experience, and yet you will realise that 'stopping', 'remembering', 'repossessing' and 'regaining' yourself for just a few seconds is an impossible feat.

'Doing' by not doing, making things happen by being still: this is the warrior's 'watch', his wake of immobility. His apparent rest is in reality putting the world in order. It only takes three seconds. It's so simple and so powerful, but without a real understanding, it's impossible.

One, two, three…

You are here, totally. This is 'doing', this is power; this is freedom. Possessing yourself for three seconds: it's the power of *will at work*. An intentional 'will', conscious and fully aware of itself cannot be attacked by anything or anybody any more than light can be attacked by darkness.

Humanity lives by reaction, a zoological species guided by external signals, reactive to impulses coming from a world they believe to be outside of themselves. Reactivity is slavery, impotence, lack of will, lack of awareness and lack of light.

Problems are resolved from inside. When a man begins to govern himself, the world knows. When you have solved yourself, when you have stopped complaining, accusing and regretting, you've freed the world. Living the moment in its totality is the solution of all and for all.

When this victory reveals within, you feel gratitude for everyone. You want everyone to win and to be successful. When you feel this sense of bliss and certainty within, the entire world feels safe, and you can't have enemies to fight, nor antagonists or obstacles to overcome.

'In this moment, I'm in charge of myself and nothing is external'. This is not the affirmation of a presumptuous man, but the realisation of a state of awareness that makes you get up in the morning with a smile, puts you in a state of gratitude and makes you bless everyone and everything.

When you feel pain inside, you have to resolve it. You can't move until you master it. Three seconds of totality, three seconds of real power move mountains. Possessing yourself is the lever that moves the world. It's you that gives life. The external world is only but a reflection conditioned by you.

As soon as you wonder and you're distracted, you enter into an infernal machine that you yourself have created. Until there's this voice, everything goes back into place and everything finds a solution. If this voice is missing, you're lost.

A school of being should teach immobility. Real 'doing' is suspending every action until you are fully 'in charge' of yourself.

One, two, three…! You feel victory inside. One, two, three seconds, you feel victory for the first time. A second time doesn't exist. Victory is inexhaustible; there is no beginning and no end. It's always there, available, you can take advantage of it at will. What's missing is you!

Losing this state of grace, entering in the world without this victory inside means to be 'at the mercy' of your own pyramid. It's your own dependency that eliminates you, cutting you down in the same way the subjects of a kingdom would decapitate a king who no longer served them.

Three seconds to 'repossess' yourself, and you'll feel the world become lighter, memory vanishing and the instant manifesting in all its power.

You'll wish those three seconds were forever.

Before facing a battle, Lupelius's monk-warriors had to put their integrity, their impeccability to the test.

They drew aside in solitary places, remaining still in a state of suspension, of pure contemplation in order to enter into the most obscure corners of their own beings. In those few moments of silence, their enemy would appear from the darkness in all his cruelty, and only then did the real battle take place.
Only those who would come out whole and unharmed were granted the privilege of entering the battlefield.

Their inner purity made them invulnerable in war and immortal in life.

Fearlessness

Absence of death means fearlessness, which is the very cause of all that we know as truth, beauty and goodness.
Fearlessness is the basic principle of being whole. A man of integrity is such because he has won and cancelled for good his own destructive state of fear.

Fearlessness is the supreme nature of your being; and it is your level of being which determines your history and your destiny—if you are in fear then, you will create troubles and difficulties for yourself and for others.

Remember! Fear is the very cause of all that you are afraid of, and fearlessness, the realisation of all that you can dream of.

Men are placed at various levels on an invisible ladder according to the level of the inner responsibility they have acquired.

Organisations limit themselves to the acknowledgement of such levels, which have been universally assigned to each man, like paints of different hues that colour the sides of pyramids otherwise invisible.

By observing an individual or an organisation, everyone can perceive immediately the *dimension of having*; a few and with more difficulty can perceive the *dimension of doing*—but the *dimension of being*, the depth of ideas, values and 'dream' that is behind every individual and organisation, the real cause for their abilities and their destiny, remains invisible.

Possessions, energies, material goods and resources of any kind are only an effect, the projection of the ability to *do*. In return, doing and having as a dichotomy depend on the being just like a shadow depends for its dimension and form on the object that is projecting it.

If, until the third millennium threshold, the dominant thought and the prevailing conception of our whole civilisation has been 'to have in order to do and therefore to be'. It is time to turn it upside down and to take part in the revolution. A man, a civilisation, a country, have the ability to do and to own only what they have already achieved in their being; events and circumstances in their history and all they meet, whether good or bad, has a perfect correspondence to their level of being, to the breadth of their ideas, to the profoundness of their values.

In nature, as well as in economics, every recovery proceeds from the inside to the outside, from the invisible to the visible, from being to having.

The success of any enterprise depends mainly upon the inner responsibility and integrity of their leader. Many organisations have failed because of lack of an intrepid leader, pragmatic Dreamer and philosopher of action.

The training of a leader through self-knowledge leads him to the dream that every man has buried in the innermost recesses of his being.

A leader is always in a state of alertness. Moving up continually, he can never stop.

Until now, all economic systems have dealt with survival, with peoples' basic needs: food, shelter, clothing and reproduction—the economics of Neanderthals and the economics of a modern complex society are essentially the same.

The new economics of the coming decades will deal no more with survival or with keeping people alive for a few decades, but with longevity and everlasting life, it is the beginning of a twenty-first century *Economics of Immortality.*

In the past, economy has been based on calculation, programs, plans and mathematics, but mathematics cannot deal with qualities, only with quantities. If you live in a merely quantitative universe, nothing is possible for you, neither change nor transformation, because transformation is a question of quality.

The financial crisis that systematically seems to be scourging our Economy is only the disastrous effect of a loss in your inner being. What you personally are going through is not a financial crisis, but a crisis of values.

Any time you have difficulty making an important decision, you can be sure that it is the result of being unclear about your values. In a qualitative economy, the amount of efforts is insignificant in comparison with the quality of efforts. Money like love is an inner matter. Money is a state of being. Money-affluence manifests in time what you have conquered through inner responsibility and creative victory, which is love. In the same way, any fault in your being makes you weaker and poorer.

Any crack in your vision shatters the foundations of your financial power.

All conflicts, wars and financial crisis, are reflecting the inner conflict of man.
It is there where we have to intervene.

This is the economics to come. Industries and corporate enterprises will soon teach the *Art of Dreaming*, the principles of self-improvement and inner integrity, to enable their people, managers and employees, to grow and become advanced beings.

The world of business has to realise that real, financial expansion comes out of quality and declines rapidly when quality is missing.

One day, all organisations, from the smallest businesses to the huge multinationals, will have at their helm a philosopher of action, a pragmatic Dreamer, a luminous visionary who has taken care of his own integrity, who knows how to believe in the impossible and make it concrete.

Organisations, as individuals, must realise that their development and prosperity does not depend on the outside world, but on their own inner qualities, values and ideas.

You

Artificial intelligence, robots and automation are said to completely replace and render obsolete the way that mankind works and produce today. What do you envision will be the work of the future?

The Dreamer

We are rapidly moving towards a not-doing civilisation where truth, goodness, beauty and the pursuit of happiness are the pillars of a shining new economically evolved society.

One day a dreaming society will no longer work. A humanity that loves will be rich enough to dream and infinitely rich because it dreams.

It's a new era of Golden Creative Leisure!

The broader a man's vision, the richer his economy. This holds true for an organisation, a country and an entire civilisation.

The destiny of the business, and all that it has gained in years and years of activity, is intertwined with the figure of its founder, and even his own physical integrity. Big businesses, entrepreneurial fortunes, like nations and entire civilisations, form and prosper, or take ill and die, with their leader, with their founder-creator. An organisational pyramid is tied to the breath of its leader. If the leader is well and prospers, so will the company.

All of our thoughts, emotions, fantasies, memories and imaginings and above all our dreams, are part of a world that is intangible and parallel to what we have learned to interpret as existence.

An organisation is a living being, and the most subtle of its components, its ideas, values and fundamental beliefs, all come from its invisibility and it is the invisibility of its men, in particular the founder, his own level of being and understanding, that determine its success and financial destiny.

Behind the values of a man lies his 'dream'. A man that has no 'dream' is destined to decay under the weight of social conflicts and of economic crisis.

At the time of a great financial crisis, many bankers, businessmen and stockbrokers 'crash' because they totally identify with the failing economy. In what should be a marvellous game of creativity and intuition, they instead are hypnotised to the point that they no longer realise to be the players and not the pawns, the observers and not the observed, the Dreamers and not the dreamed.

They depend upon external conditions to plan their strategies, and rely upon budgets, reports and financial forecasts to unconsciously build nothing more than a house of cards.

Problems exist to reveal the inner limits and suffering that you have unconsciously imposed upon yourself.
Remember! What you call problems are only solutions not yet recognised travelling fast towards an imminent fortune.

Get into trouble… 'intentionally'.
Push yourself to the brink of the abyss, 'firmly trusting' your intuition and integrity. The problems and difficulties you suffer and that apparently overwhelm you, will be instantly resolved if you 'deliberately' expose yourself to issues and responsibilities of a higher order.

You

You said that a financial crash is only a consequence of an inner crack, which has devastating repercussions on our physical body, our family, our business and the entire world. It seems impossible to imagine that even the slightest lowering within myself can create such a great disaster.

The Dreamer

Man cannot hide. The world knows everything about you. You can evolve or degrade at any moment.

It's up to you. Each of your thoughts, attitudes, words and glances, even the slightest grimace denounces to the entire universe your level of responsibility and freedom.

This is what unmistakably places you where you are and determines your destiny, financial status and role in the theatre of existence.

You

There have been many leaders, revolutionaries, philosophers, visionaries, reformers, dictators, popes, kings and emperors, who have attempted to change or improve the life of man, but none have ever succeeded. Why is that?

The Dreamer

They didn't succeed because they tried to change man through external means such as religions, disciplines, education, politics, physical and psychological pressure, external knowledge and technology. Even at present time people believe that man can be changed solely by education, and that higher education for everybody will solve all problems.

If you believe in the external world as something objective, then you are destined to fail. The world that you see and touch is only a pale shadow of your subjectivity, a fancy projection of your inner being. Therefore, any attempt to change the world through external devices—science, technology, education, religion or politics will only perpetuate and aggravate humanity's sufferings and sorrow. Your age-old illusory belief that something is going to change in time, will cast you into the self-created prison of ignorance and dependency.

A real change can only happen through an educational revolution coming from within, turning your vision upside down and acknowledging you yourself as the sole Dreamer and creator of the entire universe.

The richness of a man, the economy of a company as well as the financial destiny of a nation are the result of their philosophy, of their ethical values and of their convictions. In the near future, every company will have an ideology, a philosophy which accounts for its success and longevity; at the very top of every organisation there will be 'philosophers of action', visionary men and pragmatic dreamers who are able to enter the invisible world, the roots of their organisation.

Any organisation of the future will be ideological and will know that economy is the art of dreaming and that it is the system of beliefs of a man which accounts for his possibilities of knowing, doing and having. The main quality of future leaders will not be their shrewdness, their knowledge of the markets, or business acumen; but will be the capacity of harmonising opposites and transforming the adversities in events of a higher nature.

At the root of any achievement of humanity, be it social or scientific, there is always the dream of a man, only one, an individual who has believed in his dream and has put his life at stake to make it come true. Is the visible world that is born from the invisible one; in the same way that sound is born of silence and movement of stillness.

Quantum physics is revealing to us the immense empty spaces existing among the elementary particles of substance; and as such, we must explore the idea that the whole universe is composed of empty spaces and that what we call reality is made out of nothing. The rapid evolution of scientific knowledge is now itself systematically contradicting the sensible experience derived from our senses, and revealing to us that existence is only an illusion, just a virtual reality that everything that we can see, perceive, touch, feel—reality in all its variety, is merely the projection of a world invisible to our senses.

We are surrounded by invisibility and, in a world made of invisibility, we ourselves are invisible. Our thoughts, emotions, feelings, secrets, doubts, anxieties, likes and dislikes are invisible—every important thing about a man is invisible. It is the same in economy and business; there is a vertical dimension which remains invisible to most. The economy is a way of thinking, with economic facts depending on causes deriving from a superior order and being, for good or bad, the effect of moral values and system of beliefs.

The wealth of some nations as well as the underdevelopment of others cannot in fact be explained by economics. There is something in the invisibility of a country, of an organisation, of a man, in the very roots of their project which explains what we can observe in their lives.

'Visibilia ex Invisibilibus'—the visible is produced by the invisible.

As the blueprint precedes the physical construction, the wealth of a country's economy, the maturity of its institutions, the harmony of the civil and the political cannot be explained by economics.

Humanity has forgotten the laws of richness and how to prepare visionary men able to create richness. They've forgot that wealth is always a consequence of the awareness of prosperity, and that believing in limited resources is the true cause of poverty. Resources are not limited! It is man's psychology that has been educated to perceive such limits. The universe has in fact plentiful resources, with every man capable of having all that which he requires if only he can 'dream it'.

Try to hold the largest thought you can have.
For how long can you hold it? This is the measure of your own being, of your inner responsibility, and externally, of your financial destiny.

The economy is the reflection of our way of thinking and feeling, of our convictions, and of our system of values. As long as the psychology of man remains ill, then war, poverty, crime and pain will continue to be the founding pillars of the world's economy. That is why there is a thriving economy of AIDS, an economy of war and an economy of poverty; that is why today's economic system is almost a criminal enterprise. Up to now, economic prosperity has come from conflict, war, destruction and egotism; with illness, criminality and poverty giving rise to an economic machine that provides work for billions of people and, as a consequence, our economic system can't do without criminality, illness and poverty. It only pretends to defeat them, but in fact, it lives off them; it desperately needs them in order to survive.

The Second Education

Humanity thinks and feels negatively and therefore any aspiration towards a better world will not be successful without an individual revolution and only education can do it.

The first move on the path towards integrity is to escape the tyranny of the first education—which is the description of the world, and for the 'Second Education' to appear in all schools and universities and give new directions to the world about economics and financial power. An education that will teach that all comes from within—that all that you see and touch, right or wrong, good or evil, is just a projection of an invisible, powerful world, that abides right inside you.
Ordinary man is not used to following his intuition, nor is he encouraged to do so. Since ancient times, young men have been entrusted to schools at a very early age to instil and keep alive in them the pathway to that precious 'knowledge' already lying deep within them.
From the time of Socrates to modern day, these schools have existed, if somewhat secretly, all over the world—fostering and conserving for posterity the most precious treasure known to man—his innate independence.

The cells of this new humanity must be educated one by one. The harmonisation of opposites has to take place in every man; in economics as in politics. A new generation of leaders—a decision-making aristocracy, has to appear on the horizon of the world; men free from every ideology or superstition that will be able to ferry mankind from the psychological shore of the ordinary, weak, irascible and bigoted man, to that of the new man inspired by the principles of a School of Being.
All schools and all universities of the world perpetuate and spread the old way of thinking. Legions of young people prepared in schools without love and without freedom, add themselves every day to the sad army of the adults and perpetuate the professions and the roles available in an economy fuelled by pain and fear. There is no school that teaches its students how to discover and reveal the real cause of all and everything—their own being. Nowhere are they taught how to bring out their own dream and will, how to keep one's inner states free and in harmony, one's body healthy, one's very life…safe. A school of being should teach individuals how to study and observe themselves. A school of being should convey in every person this very principle: 'the world is as it is because you are as you are and not vice-versa'. However, everything that really counts and matters in life is not taught in conventional schools and universities. They are worthless and deleterious… Schools should support children and young adults to keep their own dream alive, to become free from any conditionings coming from outside and capable to lead their own life through self-awareness and will, inner understanding and love.

It is time for schools and universities to prepare economists who will be able to change the current dying systems and create a new man without destructive thoughts and negative feelings. A new generation of leaders whose economic laws understand that every conquest in the visible, every development in the capability of accomplishing and doing has always been anticipated by a conquest in the being.

The invisible dimension of ideas, the world of causes, runs vertically to man's history: scientific knowledge and technological progress proceed at the same rate with the knowledge that man has of himself and the level of inner responsibility reached.

To be is to have.
To have more, you have to be more.

The new man is already here; intelligence and love already exist in every man, we have only to eliminate the old education. It's an inside-outside process: from the individual to society.

Remember! Only the individual can transform society; only the individual, by produce truth, beauty and goodness in his inner being, can free the world from conflicts, limitation, injustice and death.

Real knowledge can only come from within.

Learning is time, and whatever is in time or ruled by time, is false. Learning is meaningless in the presence of will, and memory is as useless as learning, because your very nature, purpose and goal is creating, and creating happens only in this omnipotent everlasting moment and not in time.

The more you allow yourself to be nourished by the light of self-knowledge, the healthier you become, the freer, the wealthier, the younger, the more alert, the more alive and the more active.

This process of learning can take you years of preparation and study, daily efforts and discipline, years of trial and error, commitment and challenge, pain and wonder and yet your very goal, which is integrity, can only be achieved in this very instant…right now…if you only want it.

Thoughtlessness

'Concepts and thoughts, get rid of them, if just for a few seconds. It's the greatest power, the greatest knowledge.
It's the ignorance that knows everything'.

If you think, you sink.
Real freedom is freedom from all thoughts. Thought is distortion, interference—because it comes from the outside and therefore belongs to the illusory, to the past.

Through thought, you cannot destroy the world-description that the thought has created and that you so strenuously believe in, so you are caught in a vicious circle. The only substitute for thought which can transfer you into the absence of thought and descriptions that is inner silence is thoughtlessness.

You can enter into thoughtlessness only through attention and awareness, and that can never come as a result of practice, or a technique, which is again thought. Thoughtlessness is a state of being in which you live in observation of your thoughts, free from identification, a state in which you can transcend the game of opposites and enter into a zone where there is no antagonism. Where there is no 'yes' and 'no', and no thought.

We have lived until now thinking that thought is useful but behind our thoughts, there is something much stronger: silence.

Silence is the real doing. Silence creates and only what is created in silence will last.

Your actions are governed by the very time you are lost in them, and there, shrouded in darkness, you cannot create anything that is permanent. You will find whatever is created in time to be evanescent: alien and false. Your apparent reality will change, as you do, like a leaf blown in the wind of your very own identification.

Only by living moments of suspension can you create from inside. Here in timelessness, where you have defeated death, you can create something lasting.

Throughout the day, there seems to be continuous movement: billions of people in motion, interacting, competing, deals being made, goods being exchanged, markets rising and crushing, but in reality, things only happen because there is a suspension and a silence that permits them.

In the midst of swirling galaxies, there is a stillness, an actionless action that touches the foundations of the universe.

Then let life become a masterpiece: your own original creation.
Whatever situation you come to face in life, no matter how insurmountable the obstacle or how fierce the antagonist appears, don't be conditioned nor affected by

anything happening in the outside world. Know that you yourself have created those hypnotisms that hold you prisoner.

If you could truly and totally realise this, you will know that there is no effort you have to make to transform things, but only the patience to stay there and watch and observe this distance that grows within you. This is the secret: To resolve any problem, you have to simply return to yourself. In reality, only solutions exist, success upon success, one victory after another.

Remember that the world is not something you 'live in', but is a product and reflection of your very being. When you master yourself, the world dreams and breathes. When you indulge instead, the world will accuse and denounce your distraction by manifesting a reality that seems without balance, like a top that has stopped spinning.

You have apparently strived all your life to achieve greater knowledge, wealth and success, but expecting, like desiring or mere waiting, is negative. The world will not give you what you believe you want but the very opposite: the manifestation of your state of expectancy, which is a prison.

Knowledge and wealth cannot be acquired but only projected. Knowledge and wealth are an inalienable part of your being—they are your own being in action. You can submit yourself to every effort and discipline, from the most gruelling abstinence to the most impossible fast, only to realise that you can know and become only what you already are—to know more, you have to be more.

Only the 'dream' can make you free and make you overcome all your limits. Only the 'dream' can transform poverty into prosperity, difficulties into intelligence and fear into love. Remember this. Be aware and focused inwardly, and you'll see the miraculousness of the things that happen.

Breathe life inside, create space within yourself and in thoughtlessness, create the very world you are dreaming.

Money Is a Rubber Band

Money is a rubber band that you can stretch or compress at will. Money, like any other resource is produced by being and obeys the elasticity of the being. The trap is in believing that there is something that exists outside of yourself. All that you want to explain outside of yourself becomes insignificant, illusory and contradictory.

Money is only a by-product. You will find all the resources you need if you don't let the outer world to take over. So go back to the dream and win the battle, which is only with yourself. Let wealth-consciousness to take place within you, and all the financial problems will instantly disappear.
It is not the lack of money that determines your limits and constrictions. But vice versa, it is your inner limits and misery that determine your lack of resources and financial misfortune.

For a man of integrity, the new man, doing precedes thinking or planning, the solution precedes the problem and victory precedes the battle, so that the latter disappears.

This Is Economics

If you were to find an object, even if it were a jewel studded with diamonds, your first thought should be to give it back, to deliver it immediately!

That object is there to measure you; it is a measuring stick of your life, of your worth. It buys you and it sells you. Only a dishonest person or someone who is about to become a dishonest person can find an object. A man destined to become rich doesn't find anything by chance. He builds his wealth: this is economics.

If you find an object, don't even think about making it yours because that object would destroy you; one lifetime wouldn't be enough to pay for it.

To find an object or money is a trick to test you because you don't know yourself. That object could tempt you or buy you. Even just thinking about making it yours would make you fall into an area of crime where you would be stuck for decades.

Those who are meant to be rich become so through their own efforts and ideas, through their own dream. Even just buying a lottery ticket or betting money just once at a gambling table means showing signs of impotence, of distrust of yourself; it means excluding yourself from health, from prosperity, from power and from happiness. It puts you out of the game. You have already lost!

You have traded the immense power to do things using your own strength with the false hope of winning. This makes you enter into an inferno of addiction, of fear, of poverty; into an area of crime, of unhappiness, of shame. Observe them well. The players are all irresponsible addicts. A gambler is an employee who doesn't have the strength to support wealth. He cannot deserve to become rich, and that is why everything always goes against him. Placing a bet is the exposure of your incapability to be generous, to be responsible or to love. This is economics.

A man destined to become rich doesn't find anything by chance. He builds his wealth.

Never forget: whoever finds a precious object is dishonest; that object that you think you found by chance is there to buy you. It is saying: "I will buy you, I will reveal your true nature, your true worth. I will show you that which you don't know about yourself: that you are a criminal and that you aren't ready to become responsible, independent and rich."

So be careful… A person who believes in himself and in his capabilities never finds anything. Even finding it means that you are corruptible; that you are already a thief. Even only thinking about keeping it opens a wound that will continue to bleed and will take years to heal. No one can tell you this, but whoever applies these principles to his/her own life creates wealth and prosperity without limits.

Love yourself inside, this is economics!

If you think it is foolish to act abundantly when the evidence for scarcity is all around you, do it anyway. Act as you were in possession of all that you need for a moment and then the next moment and the next.

Before any solution, comes our change.

In solitude, a true leader finds solutions, decides things and overcomes impossible issues, in silence, he wins battles and conflicts and in stillness, he climbs mountains and crosses oceans. He never asks for anything because he knows that no help can come from outside. He knows that within himself he's got all the capacity and power to attract all the resources he needs. He knows that the only tool necessary for his success is his own inner integrity.

Remember! The one who knows how to produce intentionally in himself the slightest change in his being can move mountains and projects himself like a giant in the world of events.

So intervene on your being, on the quality of your thoughts, on your ways of feeling; circumscribe your negative emotions, stop identifying with the outer circumstances, stop blaming the others, finding faults and complaining; if you rise above the clouds of fears, worries and anxieties, not only will you modify your attitude and therefore your way of reacting to the events, but you will also change the very nature of the events itself.

Only a man capable of betting everything on himself, only a man who dreams and 'wants', who asks and tries to change himself with all his forces, can make it. And even if to the eyes of ordinary humanity, he appears to be hell-bent, egotistical or cynic; a man firmly guided by his own integrity is secretly and silently conveying his inner care and love to the entire world. Accompanied by his sense of certainty, he knows that in reality he is not risking anything.

So do not fear debts and creditors. They are part of the game that you yourself have put in act. Debts are nothing more than credits not yet recognised. Don't be afraid and don't be worried! Look after your integrity and your inner impeccability.

Remember! No one can take on a debt he has not already paid and no one can have more credit than debts incurred.

In business, as in any undertakings that appear as reckless, he who has this certainty cannot be attacked, cannot fail. Whatever he touches grows richer and multiplies; under any circumstance, even the most desperate, he always finds a solution because he himself is the solution.

When you realise that your inner economy is the answer and the solution to all crisis, and that external wealth is nothing but an extension of that very inner economy, you will see revealed a tremendous power within you that will change and govern the world at will, in harmony and prosperity.

'The slightest change in your being moves mountains in the world of events'.

The Fleeting Moment

Just before waking up from sleep, there is a fleeting moment of absolute freedom: no past no future, no memory nor imagination. It's a timeless state of ecstasy that if entered into consciously, if made permanent would bring everything into perfect order and justice, and will release limitless supplies and infinite resources to fulfil all your expectations in life as well as in your businesses and activities.

You

How can a science as practical as economy be governed by something as intangible as the Art of Dreaming?

The Dreamer

Economy is the Art of Dreaming, the ability to transform the impossible into possible and then into inevitable.

The first lesson of any class of economics begins with this statement: 'Resources are limited, and economics is the science that teaches how to manage them'. In truth, the resources are not limited and are by no means the main obstacle to the development and well-being of the society. The real stumbling stone is humanity as we know it; it is the psychology of man. The conviction of the limited resources available leading to affirm that if any country can be rich, most of the other countries must be poor.

This idea is so entrenched in every human being that it turned out to be a second nature, a kind of consciousness of scarcity that accompanies you, which gives shape to your thinking and guides all your choices. The truth is that the real condition of poverty and limiting more worrying is the lack of men able to bear the responsibility of a dream of prosperity, broad and creative ideas to believe in with all your strength paying the price in advance.

You

If, as you say, resources are limitless, how come there are more than three billion people that are suffering from starvation?

The Dreamer

The reason our world has three billion people starving and in deprivation is the result of an imposed belief based on a monetary, quantitative economy. Starvation and poverty will disappear from the earth if we understand that solution can only come from an inner creative economy.

But you have to remember that freedom, justice and prosperity for all humans is a romantic illusion when it is believed or expected coming from outside.

Freedom and prosperity are the outcome of a healthy humanity that understands that 'nothing is external' and that only a creative, qualitative economy coming from within can save the world from war, injustice, hunger and misery.

Integrity in Action

Freedom and prosperity are the inner states of a healthy being, a man of integrity who has realised that nothing is external.

Integrity is so difficult to attain because it is impossible to become what you already are. Integrity is nothing other than the knowledge of yourself as the only one.

Integrity in action is your mission and purpose. The solution to any problem is not in casting blame or finding fault in others, but rather in rediscovering your own forgotten integrity.

Integrity is a state of being and as such, you only have the capacity to know how it has been compromised or lost. Fear, for example, disconnects you from the source of your own vitality.

Integrity means a sense of certainty, coherence and fearlessness. Integrity is a physical experience. You can feel it in your flesh and your bones, in your breath and in your heart. Integrity has powerful applications in the realm of action. Companies, governments and nations guided by men of integrity are those that are successful, profitable, happy and everlasting.

A man of integrity is a force of nature, he has always another ocean to cross or some other mountain to climb, and is never out of the game.

This is the real essence of man, a being bound by neither limits, nor conditions, by neither authorities, nor particular systems, nor fixed ideals and therefore, a totally free being: 'The *alone* that becomes *all-one*'.

Victory is now and not in time. Time in its apparent infinity is only an infinitesimal fraction of now. Your intentional return to the instant creates a small shock within—a small great victory, which will sublimate your vision, enrich your life and entirely change your history and destiny. All that you are seeking, desiring, hoping, wishing, expecting, all that you need, strength, fame, power, success, possessions, solutions, healing, knowledge or understanding, all come from within. Everything is inside yourself and nowhere else.

In this very moment, you have the key for opening the doors of victory.

You

How can I possibly be the creator of the entire world and everything that happens within it? How can I control whether a flood hits a city, or an entire region is destroyed by drought? Do I have the power to decide whether the sun will rise, or the rain will fall?

The Dreamer

The idea that you can alter and transform the unbending forces of the universe appears to the average people as arrogant, downright and unreal.

You project yourself 'out there' and then believe that that projection has a life of its own. Then you go through life reacting to one conditional circumstance after another forgetting your very nature as Dreamer and owner of the reality you are living in.

But remember, you are the one who creates his own reality, and the only one who can change it. No god can do it for you.

You

Can the Dreamer be dreamed? Can the seer be seen? Can the object see the subject?

The Dreamer

Without the Dreamer, there is no world. Without the seer, there is no seen. Without the subject, there is no object.

The 'Yes' Attitude

No birth, no death.
No beginning, no end. No history, no destiny.
No time, no space. No guilt, no split, no limit.
No past, no future.
No memory, no expectation.
No fear, no doubt, no worry.
No pain, no claim. No name, no fame, no strain.
No sin, no fault, no mean. No anger, no hatred, no regret.
No hope, no help, no need.
No planning, no complaining, no measuring.
No self-piety, no self-justifying, No self-victimising, no self-sabotaging.
No dependency, no addiction, no identification. No outer knowledge, no culture, no training, no discipline.
No politics, no nations, no religions.
No cults, no occults.
No idols, no gods.

When you have learnt how to be in prosperity consciousness, money and health, financial power and love will come to you naturally.

Chapter VII
The Body

Whatever happens in your body happens to the world. The world is as you are, and you are this body:

this birthless-deathless body.

Your physical body has to become the most pleasurable place to be so that the miraculous, the inconceivable, the most wondrous can manifest before your very eyes.

There is a blueprint of immortality in your body which you have to keep alive and active all the time.

Human beings have always believed that they were impotent and helpless on this earth and that they needed a higher power to face the challenge of life, but they didn't know what that source really was.

They always rejected the body, and searched elsewhere for the answer. They climbed mountains, crossed oceans, went to the east and to the west, met with gurus, shamans, scientists and masters—to know about the secret of everlasting life. And the answer was always the same: Stop dying! Every instant you compromise with the external, you die a little. So free yourself from all the ties that bind you, and get rid of the idea that death is invincible.

You have to realise that physical immortality is the true state and that death is a lie, that the body is indestructible and made to live forever.

If you were not dominated by the belief system that physical death is inevitable and beyond your control, you would yield a natural youthing process.

Cells never have to die! In every moment, you can inject immortality into yourself and those around you. Express immortality to yourself and those around you. Never die inside, never die in your body. In order to win death, you have to cultivate the idea that the body is indestructible, and that death is not inevitable. And so, you have to apply the principles of inner integrity and fearlessness to your physical body and learn thus the reverse-ageing process the same way you have learned the ageing-dying process.

To be physically immortal means to stop death working in your own body, to do that you have to eliminate its possibility completely from all your cells. Physical immortality means living in the now without limits, without beginning and without end. Physical immortality means taking responsibility for your flesh and making your stand now to keep it forever. It means never dying and never degrading. It is not that you become invulnerable or indestructible, but that you leave no space in yourself for death in any form.

The issue is not being alive; it is being so alive that you cannot die!

Feel yourself living forever rather than living for death. Physical immortality is the only alternative to death. You have the right to live to your full capacity without limitations or disease, poverty, ageing or death.

We are here to become immortal; this is our only real occupation.

The idea that death is inevitable casts your inner being into the unescapable prison of fear, self-destructiveness, pain, misery and failure.

It causes disease and consumption of your physical body, projects violence, persecution and war into the world around and is the very source of all cruelty, human degradation and death itself.

Remember! Man is a self-developing organism; he contains within himself all the power to produce a complete new body and project in the world of events a brand-new reality.

He has to take on immortality as his own nature and true heritage.

To live forever, you must be willing to constantly explore the unknown within.

It is not by some great work or deed that you become physically immortal; you are 'physical immortality'! You just have to wake up to who you really are. There is no struggle, hardship or suffering you have to go through to become greater. That is another lie of death.

The purpose of your life is to sustain the entire universe in comfort, order, pleasure, health and peace. You are the root of the universe. The entire world is filled with your creative energy, healing intelligence and immortality.

But heaven on earth cannot be realised as long as society, politics and economics are a creation and projection of your fragmented, violent being. Through self-government, you can govern and control governments, wars, military armaments, police, revolutions and bring peace, joy, health and prosperity to all people in the world.

The world is neither real nor unreal, neither good nor bad, neither happy nor unhappy, neither in war nor peace. The world is simply all that you want it to be.

Deathlessness has to be the only principle guiding the new man. The new man will have no creed, no faith, no religion, but deathlessness has to be his law and understanding has to be his order.

Without religion, without politics, the entire planet will be filled of peace, intelligence, silence and love. The economy of your personal energy-body is the key to physical health and world's justice, peace and prosperity.

*Every disease is a healing process that teaches you something special. Every disease contains in itself the seed of greater benefit.
Every disease is a further step towards a higher order of responsibility. Each disease hides the secret of youthing and longevity.
Each disease is an inner victory which brings you closer to realise that 'living forever' is not only possible, but inevitable.*

You

How can I 'have it because I love it'? I've been sick for two years now; they've diagnosed me with cancer.
I have travelled and met all kind of doctors, healers and shamans. I've been through all kinds of therapy to get rid of it.
Are you saying that I wanted this to happen to me? That I wanted to be sick with cancer?

The Dreamer

You are not sick with cancer. Your real sickness is more serious; it is arrogance, hypocrisy, forgetfulness.

Your mind is filled with the ballast of years and years of wrong thinking and negative emotions. You blame others for your apparent misfortune, still believing that the world 'out there' is an objective reality and that you are the victim of forces beyond your control.

You fail to see the real causes of your condition deep within yourself and therefore to understand that no help can ever come from something or someone outside yourself.

Cancer is not an illness but the cry of a man who has lived his entire life in a state of forgetfulness, inner fragmentation and absence of love.

You
What should I do?

The Dreamer

Abandon everything and think only of saving yourself from yourself. You come here to die to yourself, to face your own lies and you do not know when, or if, you will go back where you came from.

You have spent your whole life, years and years of sacrifice and exasperated effort, to end up in this condition. You have moved mountains to get this close to eliminating yourself. You could say you are a man who succeeds in failing, in killing himself. The world is full of phantoms like you.

Observe yourself! Look how satisfied you are as you add your drops of medicine into a glass of water, as you gulp down some pills. How ostentatiously you let the ones around you, your family, friends and colleagues watch you. Observe your joy as you go on your pilgrimage to the doctors, to ancient and modern medicine men, searching for a cure that you don't want.

Men like you, for a long time, have chosen death as the way out, but death is never a solution. You should never avoid, suppress or deny the trying condition of sickness; instead, accept it as a healing power and use it for your inner work of transformation.

You came here looking for a miracle, for someone that could take you out of your dying condition, but no help can come from outside. Healing is an act of will and no prayer or penitence can substitute it.

You

Who are you to tell me these things?

The Dreamer

Nobody.

Only a 'nobody' can say these things.

As you are now it is difficult to accept what I'm saying, but one day, when all lies will disappear from your inner being, you will discover that all the problems and strife in the world are merely the projection of a fallen, degraded vision, symptom of your forgotten state of integrity.

If you make the effort each day, if only for a few minutes, to align yourself with my words, and let them flow through you, you will be amazed at how easily you will overcome all the 'apparent' hardships and difficulties that life has in store.

The World Is the Symptom

The world is a symptom, your body is a symptom; everything happens to balance you.

The eternal conflict, the game of opposites, you see playing out in the world of events is merely the product of your identification and lack of awareness. The vertical man knows how to use this apparent friction between opposites; he knows that the extremes are not separate. They are two sides of the same reality.

It is this friction between opposites that creates energy that can be used as fuel to reach completeness, to reach unity of being. Instead of recognising this, the smallest trace of conflict, of war within yourself, confuses you, distracts you and eliminates you. Your negative emotions manifest themselves as tragic events, because you justify them; because you are not aware of what is happening within you emotionally and, still earlier, psychologically.

Financial crises, disease and accidents occur to balance this lack of consciousness, lack of attention, lack of self-knowledge.

So stop identifying yourself with one of the extremes or you will continue to be trapped in an illusion—in the symptom!

To make the change, to start the healing process you have to back to the real cause: yourself.

Think how revolutionary the idea, and how much effort is necessary to see every opposition, even a war, as a reflection of an unrecognised inner conflict.

So, don't alarm yourself for nothing. The more menacing the symptom, the easier it is to get a bull's eye, because the trail is deeper, more evident.

Remember! The world does not produce symptoms, it is 'itself' the symptom!

The Body and the world are one and the same thing

What is it that the world 'wants you to see' that you don't want to see or touch within yourself? Go out and see what you are lacking! If you are conscious of something negative, conflictual, obscure in yourself, that very thing will disappear. Unawareness is the real evil…that constant inner conflict that you are incapable of recognising reproduces itself outside of you as tragic, negative events; but these events only come to make you aware of your inner states; they are not a punishment but an opportunity, a blessing.

Self-knowledge is an incredibly powerful *magic*!

Self-knowledge means not allowing even an atom of darkness in your being. It is only when you refuse to meet that darkness within yourself, when you leave it unchecked, that it manifests and becomes visible in the outside world as symptoms that you then perceive as an invasion, an attack, an insult.

Self-knowledge, self-remembering, self-consciousness is light that enters into your being and puts things in order. If what you observe within yourself remains, then it is real, if it disappears it is not real.

Remember! In the body, as in the world, we receive symptoms as the last signals of something missing, lacking and of something incomplete which is crying for completeness, which is crying for unity, for healing, for perfection.

Disease and accidents are the extreme, final signals to show you the way back to integrity.

We ourselves allow this body to be destroyed. The very thoughts and feeling we impose upon the body are creators of ageing disease, failure and death. Whatever happens in your body happens to the world. The world is as you are, and you are this body: *this birthless-deathless body.*

> *There is no incurable disease except those you*
> *acknowledge to be such.*
> *There is no situation in life that cannot be changed if you realise that you yourself*
> *are the source of all that*
> *happens to you.*

The ultimate aim of illness is healing. The illness is pointing out the way to happiness, certainty, security, safety

The symptoms are signs that indicate the path to healing. The illness is the cure. Any attempt to eliminate the symptom, as all medicine does, is ignorance; along with the symptom, the opportunity for a superior cure is eliminated.

Cutting out a gland or an organ through surgery, is a crime. Cutting out a part of the body when it is inflamed is like removing a fire detector because you don't like to hear it ring every time there is a fire. Live with your pain, study it, learn from it, keep it close like a friend and listen to its counsel.

Even cancer is a cure. The question is not of conquering cancer but of understanding it, so that you can understand yourself.

You have no disease, only your abominable thoughts and this death that you carry inside you and spread all around you. Your desire for annihilation darkens your world and makes it sick. There is nothing easier to cure than that which you call cancer. But for manufacturers of disaster, prophets of doom like you, it is impossible. How can you be cured of a disease that doesn't exist? Your tumours are cracks in your being.

If you become cancerous, it's because you are cancerous. The cancer cell persists in believing in a separate outer world just as you do. This belief is fatal. And the only remedy is *a-mors*, the Latin word for *love* that is never indulging in a death attitude.

Cancer is love at the lowest level. Cancer is the symptom of misunderstood love. The symbol of true love is the heart.

And the heart is the only organ that cannot be attacked by cancer.

You

You suggest to be far away from all doctors and every kind of medicine. What should we do then when we get seriously sick?

The Dreamer

Do nothing. Just stay still, within and without. Breathe deep and fast until you feel better.

Remember! All illnesses are themselves powerful cures in process, and you shouldn't dare to stop them with any kind of external intervention.

Stay away from medicine and doctors. Healing can never come from physicians or doctors. There has never been a doctor anywhere, at any time, in any place on Earth, at any period in history who ever healed anything or anybody.

If you really want to heal, you have to first of all stop believing that death by disease or accident is natural and then question its inevitability with all your strength.

You have to become a living demonstration that disease, ageing and death are totally unnecessary.

You

And the millions of young people that are diagnosed with depression and are placed under the cure of psychiatrists and psychologists every year? How can we face the growing threat of mental illnesses in modern society?

The Dreamer

*Resorting to the use of psychology and psychiatrists in an attempt to heal and solve your problems will only worsen your condition and leave you helpless.
Depression, anxiety and all forms of mental illness are just the inventions of a primitive psychology, of a fragmented being that is possessed and ruled by a legion of negative emotions, destructive thoughts and contrasting desires that pull in opposite directions and tear him apart.*

*It is your inner fragmentation that, left unchecked, creates and projects a world of conflicts, divisions, human and natural disasters, crime and wars.
Therefore only you, in this very moment, have the power to heal, save or help yourself.*

How can you wait for anyone or anything to come and set you free, if you yourself are the liberator?

You

Why are the masses and the conventional medicine system as a whole not only impervious to what you are suggesting, but actively opposing it?

The Dreamer

All revolutionaries stand alone.
That is what revolution is about—daring to be different—having the courage to point out a new path—accepting the ridicule and judgement from others—winning all battles, within and without, through a conscious, luminous silence.

You are here to wake up and start your own revolution: a silent, secret inner revolution that only few among few have ever been able to undertake.
You are here to turn upside down the deeply-rooted belief that death is invincible.

The Cult of Death

There are many religions and cults on this planet, and many others are going to be created by man, but the largest one, the one which contains all of them, is the cult of death. It is produced by human beings who have been programmed to die. This program is the strongest force at work in your being and in your life.

The day you stop worshipping death and recognise your inner being as the sole cause of all and everything, religions and all cults will cease to exist.

Stalked by death and misery, tormented by pain and evil, you have only one way out: to find real life in the most hidden and obscure recesses of your inner being.

With the transformation of pain and suffering in your own body, you will witness the transformation of the entire world.

You
Can you tell us how we can approach life knowing that one day we are going to die?

The Dreamer
Instead of waiting for the end of your time, try to go back to your supposed beginning, and simply realise that you have never been born; and that all the past and the entire story of your life is just a projection of this very instant.

This realisation will make you whole, happier, stronger, healthier, wealthier and, more than anything, indestructible.

You

So, will humanity ever be able to overcome physical death?

The Dreamer

You ask about how to overcome physical death, but your question manifests a total misunderstanding about life and death. There is no technology, no discipline and no means, no God from outside that can help you. Simply stop believing that you were born, and death will suddenly disappear. How can you die if you are an unborn being?

Learn to live in the now.

In a state of stillness, secretly and silently, *your 'being now' will totally delete the fairy-tale of your never-happened birth and all your suffering events connected to it. Your 'being now' will transform your imaginary death and your dreary prophecy of disaster into a real powerful, everlasting, beautiful life.*

For so many years, you have looked for a saviour, for a healer. You believe in external help and protection.

You are looking to get something for nothing, not knowing that the highest price you can ever pay is to get it for free.

Instead of buying, begging or depending upon a cure, stop producing disease.

Regain your innocence, your power of healing and start to love yourself inside.

Fasting

Ordinary people only fast between meals. Some people only during sleep—with sleep being for them a form of involuntary fasting that the body forces onto itself in order to keep itself alive; but fasting, like healing, should always be an act of will.

Throughout ancient times, fasting was practiced and used by warriors not only when facing an illness, but also on the eve of an important undertaking—when faced with insurmountable odds; as by fasting, the body re-establishes its natural order following the weakening of years and years of bad habits and neglect, and in turn produces back nourishment and strength.

But man has long forgotten the self-healing nature of his body, choosing to instead resort to external means, to doctors and medicine, whenever the slightest discomfort arises.

We give ourselves wholly and without questioning to a healer or a doctor when facing an illness; when their presence should instead be forbidden, and be substituted with the understanding that it is the illness itself that brings the healing—that any external intervention with medicines or drugs will result only in a sabotage of our body's natural healing process.

It is the illness itself that heals; that shelters, protects, teaches, atones, cleanses, clears, lifts, straightens and reforms—it is the illness itself that makes us more aware and more intelligent.

The human body is a machine that regulates itself on its own: sickness is a natural function of the body; like breathing, digestion, circulation, excretion, the proliferation of cells or nervous activity, and man can never intervene upon, nor artificially substitute or stimulate, such a process trough external means.

Remember! All medicines and all the schools of healing are a fraud. All 'cures' are frauds. Doctors and their poisonous medicine cannot heal; and in the name of science, millions of patients pay every day only to be crippled and murdered.

Fasting on the other hand is not a medicine, but a suspension—a rest from the process of digestion, and man's oldest and most effective way to conserve your health. The power of creation and transmutation resides in the organs of your body, and through fasting the organism is permitted to rest and focus its own energies in other, more urgent directions; allowing for the healing to naturally take place, by simply...*doing nothing.*

There is no substitute for fasting: only the complete elimination of food for a sustained period of time, and not the mere limitation to foods such as vegetables, fruit and juices, will produce results and slow down the body's own ageing process. The closer the reduction of food is to fasting, the more benefits are gained.

While fasting, the intestines are allowed to rest, and whatever is lost, is only inversely proportional to its usefulness. You will see that useless, harmful tissues are digested by themselves and disappear, while the useful ones remain intact. Blood, purified by the work of detoxification, nourishes the brain more efficiently; giving it more clarity and sharpness—eyes and sight are strengthened and fortified, touch becomes more sensitive, hearing is improved and, in the case of old age, recovers completely.

Healthy kidneys produce fearlessness, will power and determination; creative thinking and the production of creative ideas depend upon a healthy liver, in the same way that the power of emotional logic and intuition resides in the spleen and pancreas.

Fasting is an intuitive art that takes a lot of experience to master, but is ultimately the understanding that you yourself are the healing.

Remember! The body is indestructible and is paradoxically *unhealable* because it cannot get ill. What you call illness is only part of the process of integration and any external intervention, be it surgery or medicine, means giving up the omnipotence, the indestructibility, the immortality of the body—and above all, it means an abdication of the will, of your own integrity.

The one who practices the art of *stillness and fasting* knows that the body is his laboratory, and is strong even though he feels weak.

Victory over food is the path to the 'ultimate victory'.

You

If 'nothing can come from the outside', how should one nurture oneself then? Don't we depend from the intake of external food and water in order to survive?

The Dreamer

There is nothing that a man, once returned to his integrity, needs to introduce from the outside, neither food, nor knowledge, nor happiness. It is his conquest not to depend on anything outside of himself.

Man can nurture himself from within, from his own intelligence, his own will, his own light.

You

I am very much aware and take good care about the type of food that I eat. I believe it is very important to eat organic, without any additives or chemicals. Is this not the right approach for a healthy lifestyle?

The Dreamer

When choosing food, you think and believe that it must be natural, pure and healthy. Don't worry about it anymore! You only have to be aware of it, and no longer will you need to choose food or drinks based on their nutritional value. Part of your self-sabotage program, which is a daily attempt on your life, lies in making you believe that there are fixed rules to follow.

Remember, the only food that really nourishes and sustains you, comes from your inner light and freedom.

Behind illness, accidents and death lies a dreadful boss, a tyrant that controls everything: taste.

Taste is the true master that decides the destiny of ordinary men, from crib to tomb. Taste is more powerful than any other sense or function: sight, hearing, sleep and sex. The original sin, that of Adam and Eve, was tasting external life. More than any other sense, the sense of taste, for the ordinary man, is the most difficult to overcome. It controls all his life and determines his destiny. Like animals, to feel alive we have to feel something in our mouth, we have to taste.

You are now called to invert it, to transform taste for flavours into taste for life, for eternal life, for immortality.

Victory over death is essentially victory over food.

You are convinced that death in an unavoidable event decreed by some basic scientific principle.

Religion and science have made you believe that death is a universal law coming from above and as such, impossible to change, so you cannot hope for anything better than dying.

To pursue physical immortality, you have to get rid of any knowledge coming from the outer world, including the hypnotic descriptions of your birth and death, and of the past and future, and rediscover within yourself the infinite, inexhaustible passion and commitment to the eternal now.

If you question the idea that death is inevitable, you have a chance. If you don't, you will remain prisoner of your own description and victim of your own conflictual thoughts and emotions.

Remember! Your inner conflicts and self-sabotage are more dangerous than any war. Physical death can materialise as a consequence of an infinite number of inner deaths. You have to practice to die less until one day you finally stop dying all together. You have to learn to not allow one single moment of death inside.

If you are alert, present and take more care of your inner life, there wouldn't be moments of drowsiness, tiredness and sorrow.

You are here for one reason only: to win Death. Nothing else matters.
The long agony that you call reality stops existing here.

To win death is the only game worth playing.

If you do not circumscribe your sorrow and pain, it will materialise in unpleasant events. Health, wealth and success are all projected from inside. How can you have a beautiful life, a winning personal adventure, if you die inside? Physical immortality needs self-mastery, and there is no self-mastery without healthy emotions.

When you feel insecure and uncertain, when you are afraid or feel hurt, when you accuse, blame others or regret, when you complain or self-justify, if you observe yourself more deeply, you will find out that it is always the same pain, springing from your harmful attitudes and countless inner deaths.

But you have yet to recognise this pain as the very cause of all your troubles and difficulties. Do not turn your back on anything which hurts you. Face your inner war. Look at it fearlessly and recognise it as the only way towards freedom.

Behind and beyond any belief or adventure in life, you have only one task to focus on, and this is 'victory over death'.

If your vision narrows, if your level of being lowers, then the external world, which you call reality, becomes like a mountain towering over you, until you are lost in its shadow.

That is the time when you expect something from outside to assist you, when you look for somebody to help you…when you look for certainty in the eyes of others…when you search for help, reassurance and consideration from the world.

Change your vision instead; raise it! Look at the world with a new awareness, and the entire universe will become as tiny as a grain of sand. There is no help coming from anywhere at all…you have to make your own individual revolution, which is purely based upon you. Outside you, there's no force, whether it be known or unknown, visible or invisible, that can influence your destiny. You are by yourself surrounded by wonder and infinity.

It has to be done, especially when you feel at a loss, when you are under the most difficult conditions, when existence grips you in a vice so you cannot breathe. That is your great opportunity to win death! Do not expect! Do not react! Do not identify with the world around you! Live in a state of powerful silence and stillness: a state of complete suspension.

Identifying with the world seals you in the prison of time, in an infernal circle where you are prey to your negative emotions. But when you realise that there is nothing to fear, fear itself disappears and freedom takes the upper hand. The inferno starts crumbling, flaking away layer by layer and you begin to feel alive.

Love your body and give up the idea of killing it. Do it now! Master your body! Breathe out all the plans of death, and get your body to look and feel the way and the age you want it to. Remember! It is in this body that you can heal the world. It is in this body that you can win death.

Eat less, dream more. Sleep less, breath more. Die less and live forever.

Ageing, sickness and death are insults to human dignity and yet they are the very pillars which, for thousands of years, have supported an illusory description of the world.

You

More and more people seem to turn to plastic surgery, beauty products, diets and all sorts of practices in an attempt to stop aging and turn back the biological clock. What shall it be our attitude towards this *culture*?

The Dreamer

Everyone desires to remain young forever and never get old, and as such go through all kind of disciplines, doctrines, ideologies, interventions and systems without ever realising that any method or knowledge coming from outside is an illusion and could never allow me to stay young.
To rely on external devices means to depend on chance, and that means to lose all battles you will undertake against 'time'. Whatever you win by chance, 'unfortunately' by chance, sooner or later, you will also lose it.

You can only win by will.

Will and dream are one and the same. Then remain a Dreamer and you will never lose…you will never age…you will never die.

Voluntary Death

You need to master the process of regeneration of your physical body, eliminating thus all boundaries and limitations through a remarkable technique—voluntary death.

Voluntary death means the conscious willingness to face and release all your false ideas and unpleasant emotions apparently accumulated in your body. Voluntary death prevents involuntary physical death.

You collect traumas, negative emotions and destructive thoughts in your body until it becomes such an unpleasant place to live in, that physical death appears to be the only way out.

You
When will men stop dying?

The Dreamer
When they stop believing, they were born.

You

But what you are suggesting is impossible! How would the world be if we stopped dying?

The Dreamer

It would be a very funny world, surely more alive!

Try to visualise a humanity without conflicts, wars, persecutions, diseases, poverty and injustice. Try to imagine a world without tribunals, police, prisons, hospitals and cemeteries and you will know how an intelligent, joyful, immortal humanity would live.

Remember! Immortality doesn't mean the life 'after' death, full of imaginary angels, ascensions, heavens or reincarnations, but it is about life 'without' death.

It is about life with all its infinite possibilities.

You
So, what will be the alternative to death?

The Dreamer
Living in the now.
In absence of fear and with a sense of trust, certainty and conscious control over one's inner life, that is, to stop dying within and live forever. Remember! The very killer of humanity is the idea of the inevitability of death.

Dematerialisation means to disappear from mortal eyes, that is, if you are really alive you cannot be seen by people who are ruled by death.

The art of materialising and dematerialising belongs to one who has attained inner unity. If you are whole, then you will manifest everlasting life and will be visible only to higher beings.

For the average man, the above is unknown and inexistent and if you raise the vibrations of your body, you'll disappear from his limited vision.

The story of Jesus is such because it is invented and passed on by mortal men, but his real story, that witnessed by those who have stopped dying is a whole other thing.

To believe in the birth, death and resurrection of a god-man named Jesus means empowering and perpetuating in oneself the illusion of passing time—the catastrophic mortal vision of life.

All that belongs to time is false, and false is everything that time contains. This can be understood only when the now in you—real time takes command.

It seems paradoxical, yet when you stop dying within, Real life will overwhelm you and occupy every atom of your being; you will no longer be witness to suffering, persecution or dying.

When you stop dying within, the entire world will be safe.

The world can become Heaven on Earth; it's all up to you: *the world is as it is because you are as you are.*

Jesus on the cross is the symbol of man trapped in the wheel of time. The crucifix symbolises man fixed and lost in his own self-created system of suffering and death.

It's not necessary to die to become immortal, but it is of capital importance not to be born, that means to go deeply within yourself and realise that you have never been born, that your birth has never happened and that all your past and destiny are just a self-invented story which begins and ends in this very moment.

All things subject to birth are destined to disappear. If you question then your very birth, you might discover eventually that you have never been born and that your birth is no more than a hypnotising description of reality and not reality itself—an imaginative ideological concept that you believe to be true.

To be born, you must inevitably die; therefore, to not die and live forever, you have not to be born—that means that you have to stop believing you were ever born and realise steadfastly that birth like death is only propaganda—pure superstition.

Remember! Only he who has never been born can live forever.

You

Which science, discipline or technique, amongst many, can be more effective to make us immortal?

The Dreamer

You don't have to do anything to live forever but to accept yourself as a birthless-deathless being.

If you are not immortal now, then you never will be.

Immortality is not a final destination. Immortality is not a process of growth that makes you one day perfect. If you try to improve yourself through some discipline and apply it to become immortal, you will never succeed.

Immortality cannot happen in time. Immortality is something you already are. Living forever is all about transforming the quality of your life from within, by focusing all your attention on the real cause of all and everything: the omnipresent now.

By forgetting whom you are and imagining yourself a mortal creature, you create so much trouble for yourself.

By believing that you were born and that you will die, you create and perpetuate the drama of your birth and death.

Immortality reveals when the description of death no longer has power over you.

The transformation from mortality to immortality is easier than you think. Perpetual longevity is natural, death is unnatural; that is why it takes so long to die, most people exert so much effort that it causes them illness and pain.

When you release your loyalty to death, success becomes more effortless, success in any field. All healing is temporary until we heal death. If you are dying, you are unconsciously contributing to the death of everyone around you. Once your mind and body are centred on truth and physical immortality, you have perfect peace and health.

You can never believe or achieve immortality, you can only be it. The truth is that you are always in harmony with it but you think you are not and this thought makes you miserable, and this can cause you to destroy your body.

The idea of physical immortality allows you to relax and enjoy life. It gives you time to succeed in life and achieve wealth and happiness. Only through new ideas and conscious efforts can any permanent change be produced. Only intentional, conscious work on oneself could make a man capable of surviving death.

The idea of death and death itself has been so popular for centuries because no one ever dared to question it. You are so limited that you cannot see the limits that you yourself project. You resist the idea that you can live as long as you would like to live because of your unshakable belief in death; you walk around with an underlying feeling of impending disaster and utilise distractions as an alibi to escape the overwhelming horror of death.

Your fear of death turns you towards organised religions or ideologies and distracts you from an individual path which will make you recognise that you are the one who creates his own reality. Once you take this path, you will no longer let fear, doubt or any negative emotion guide your life. You will not accept any more living in a world run by the culture of death and you will naturally abandon all forms of religion and philosophy that glorify death.

You have to realise that living is a great challenge whereas death is relatively easy. When contemplating physical immortality, it's natural to also contemplate mortality, so that you know everything about death whether or not you question it. When you will be living from a place of pure integrity and freedom, your relationship with time changes—you don't feel any more pressured to get all of your life's goals achieved quickly or staying busy so that your working hard can justify your existence.

Destroying the body by dying is an insult to the intelligence that created it, which is you yourself. Matter responds to the power of being. Will power, which is your being in action, directs energy and energy in turn acts upon matter.

The stronger the will, the greater the force of energy and the greater the energy's impact on external events and circumstances.

You

Old age has weakened my body, numbed my senses and clouded my thinking. How can I believe in immortality now, in the twilight of my life, when the prospect of death is so real?

The Dreamer

Senility is not the threshold to death, as it is commonly believed, but a way to bring up to the surface all the destructive, psychological pollution that needs to be healed and released.
This is what physical immortality is all about.
Senility has to be seen as a second childhood, consciously lived, fully alive, free from any roles, duties, plans, travels, impositions and conditions. Old age should not be resisted nor denied, but accepted, studied and mastered.

You still perceive yourself as a limited, vulnerable body that was born and a little later dies—it is an illusion. Birth and death are the symbolic manifestation of the insane, self-hypnotised human mentality.

Remember that what you perceive as real is just the materialisation in time of your inner states. The slightest change in your own being will make you project a completely different world, a new order of reality. Birth and death will then totally disappear if you allow the power of now to have the upper hand over the obsolete, dreary, self-imposed description of life.

*Death is not caused by any god or devil.
Death is caused by people who do not know any other way out of their sufferings and sorrow.*

*But death will never be the way out... Death is the way of the irresponsible.
The world as you perceive it now is limited and perishable just as you are; and only when you become responsible for your life, for yourself and understand that you can change outer life at will, you will witness life becoming a paradise.
A man of inner responsibility, of integrity; a man who perceive the real world cannot see the world of death. For death is not of the real world.*

Health, success, prosperity and happiness, are the natural expression of a conquered immortality.

You are on the threshold of the most important endeavour humanity could ever dream of: Physical immortality.

Chapter VIII
Timelessness

Now is everything. Now is eternity.
That which you are now, you always have been and always will be and yet, before now, nothing has ever happened.

Breathe deeply the omnipotence of this everlasting instant.
Only 'now' counts. The past is imaginary. There is no one and nothing else outside of 'now'.
Everything is a marvellous invention of this very instant.
There is no difference or distance between one second and one million years. They are all contained in this omnipotent, everlasting 'instant'.
The past is imaginary, history is mere imagination and historic characters are actors in a comedy written in this very instant enacting a script dictated by your own fantasy.

Only now can you do all that you imagine to have done in the past.
Only now can you be all that you believe to have been and change, only now can you have everything you believe to have had, and really possess it.

Now is the seed of the universe.

If you want to really take charge of your life, the first thing you have to do is to get free of the idea of the invincibility of death.

This means that the negative emotions held in the body have to dissolve; giving way for the timeless instant to eliminate all your fears and integrate certainty, and inject trust and pleasure into your body. Only self-awareness will let you come out of the psychological self-create prison of birth, dissolving all limits and bridging the gap between the inner world of being and the outer world of apparent reality.

Yes, even the very idea of birth is a lie!

The belief in birth makes you die. The idea of 'being born' makes you believe that life has a beginning—that's why death is inevitable.

For the hypnotic principle that 'whatever begins has to end', your belief in birth makes you die consequently.

To be endless, you have to be beginningless. To be immortal, you have to be birthless.

Try to understand what 'life with no birth' means. 'No birth' means that all your past is an imaginary story that you create in this very instant. It means that the now-moment is the sole reality that, like Chinese shadows, you project on the internal walls of a cocoon, a self-created prison that you believe to be your reality. To get free of those shadows and create a crack in the cocoon itself, you need to do long, hard work on yourself, so that you can finally transform your conflictual, dreary life into a wonderful, limitless, deathless reality.

Birth and death, like time, are just concepts, false beliefs, a story that we have made our own, forgetting that it is only a description. Remembering is imagining and imagining is remembering. Both are the 'invention' of this instant. Only in the moment, only in the now can we free our memory and enter in a non-programming state.

Learn to return home, come back to the moment! Everything is here, present in this instant. In this instant, we can set the foundations for our happiness, our beauty, for our lasting success or, at the opposite, we can command in our life a state of unhappiness and poverty. The instant is the reign of the dream and the dream is the reign of now—where there is no memory nor imagination, but only truth.

The moment is the root of the universe.
The world celebrates and rejoices with you if you rejoice. It lives if you are alive and dies if you die.

From the moment we open our eyes in the morning, our programming already begins. Our memory induces us to believe that we have a past and a future; we believe that there is a beginning and an end to everything. We are determined to believe that we are born and that one day, we will die. The world represents itself like a mirror image of this programming, of this agenda.

A Dreamer abides in timelessness. He knows that only there one can really *do*; he knows that the now is the only time-place where true change can occur; the only moment where one can win. No external planning or action can do that. Programming is the death of being.

Time cannot comprehend nor contain the infinity of this moment. Time cannot tell eternity. You need to learn to master time or it will master you! Now, in this moment, I am the richest, the happiest man in the world. Who can prevent this? What can impose a limit on something that has no limit? What makes us ignorant? What blinds our sight? What makes us so small? Poor? Moreover, unhappy? Enter into the now. Become without a past and future, maintain a state of absence like a computer that needs to be programmed. Maintain this attention in the moment; in there is life, real life, there is real success.

Journey back to your inner being. Back towards your uniqueness, your originality. Enter the external world only once you are *empty*, free from programming and agendas, without memories or expectations, without knowing what will happen. It is magic: the magic of the moment.

Encountering emptiness scares us. Silence, immobility threatens our memory, our agenda, threatens time itself. We are afraid to lose our fear! Touch the moment to find the root of all creation; you will discover that nothing exists outside the moment and that you are the only one there.

It is this realisation that permits you to build the universe, to contain it and to own it.

In a state of stillness, secretly and silently, you will totally delete the fanciful tale of your never happened birth and all the suffering events and circumstances connected to it. In a state of fearlessness, you will transform your imaginary death and your dreary prophecy of disaster into a powerful, everlasting, beautiful life.

You

You want me to believe that memory is a lie. That the past does not exist. But how can this be? How can it be, when I remember? I remember having parents, being a child, having experiences.

How can I believe in something like 'now' that barely lasts an instant?

The Dreamer

That which does not have limits cannot be governed by time.

Forget your past, remember your self. Memory and planning are primitive attributes belonging to the mass.

The real man, the doer, abides permanently in the Kingdom of Now.

All your life is happening 'now'. The world has never existed before now, and only you, in this precise instant can give it form, life and meaning.

The past is imaginary history, mere imagination. Every one you ever met in your life, every historic character you ever read about, every one you've seen in the evening news and that you believe to be so real are only actors, actors of a comedy written in this very instant. They are enacting a screenplay dictated by your own fantasy.

It's always this instant. Don't forget. Now! No instant before and none after.

You

Our parents, our place of birth, our country; these are all the founding blocks of our character and culture—who are we if not the direct result of what we come from?

The Dreamer

Believing in an imaginary self-created story where you are born in a given place, at a given time, from weak, capricious, human parents, surrounded by precarious, uncertain circumstances, and in the end, forced to live out an unknown, inescapable destiny, makes your existence painful, unbearable and mortal.

Acting instead as an actor your role in the world without identifying with it, and deeply 're-membering' what you really are, abolishes 'time and causation' and makes your life whole, invulnerable and immortal.

Now, try to feel what it means to 'be'—just to 'be', without being this or that. Dive deep within and strive to find out what you are in reality; only then, you will see your dreary life being transformed in an everlasting, beautiful adventure.

You

How can you live in the moment when every day, there are a thousand problems to solve?

The Dreamer

There are not a thousand problems to solve but only one: 'you'.
Remember! All happens here, in this everlasting 'instant', in this everlasting body. All that you are now paradoxically creates all that you have always been and all that you always will be.
In the midst of everyday activity, in the midst of any affair or business, seize the centre of your inner being and be there!
In front of you, the roll of time inexorably unfolds itself and actualises what you believe to be out of your control and understanding.

You
But what is the purpose of understanding that everything that is in time comes from a state of timelessness?
To what end?

The Dreamer
If you could understand that timelessness owns the time, then every moment you live in a state of timelessness makes you owner of the world.

You

You say that 'time' is an illusion and non-existent. Well, I would like to ask you then, what is going to happen to all of us in the next few hours, few years or in a few centuries if 'time' is, as you say, a fanciful matter?

The Dreamer

The answer I am going to give you will not satisfy your expectation but one day you will 'understand'.

There is no difference or distance between one second and one million years. They are all contained in this omnipotent, everlasting instant.
All you are right now, is not only happening in the 'next' few hours, years or centuries, but also and simultaneously in the 'past' hours, years and centuries.

You
But 'living' takes time. 'Living' happens in time. 'Living' is time, isn't it?

The Dreamer
No. True life happens only in the absence of time. Real life has neither beginning nor end, birth nor death, sorrow nor happiness—only freedom. Freedom from all bondage, limitation and hypnotism. Real life belongs to the almighty beauty of 'now' overwhelming all and everything.

Time-Worshippers

There is nothing that happens outside of 'now'. Everything happens now and 'for the first time'.

You yourself are happening 'for the first time' right now with all your personal history and destiny, people and events, your past and future, memories and expectations, fears and desires.

The closer you are to 'now', the clearer your understanding and the closer you are to your being, the more powerful your creativity and the capacity of 'doing'.

You

For what you say then, I could solve and erase all kinds of problems, difficulties, faults and debts 'right now' if I only wished?

The Dreamer

Yes.

You
Why doesn't it happen then?

The Dreamer
Because you yourself don't want it to happen.

You are a time-worshipper, and as such, you believe that only 'time' can change things. For you, 'time' is God.

Try to understand. What is really happening now is unique, original and absolute; it has never happened before and will never happen after.

All the things that you are witnessing now are the simultaneous effect of your infinite creativity that happens just once, and forever.

*You climbed mountains, forded streams,
crossed oceans and prayed in mosques, temples and churches, followed gurus and teachers, studied in schools and universities, created businesses and enterprises, and stumbled, stood up and walked again until you came to realise that all that which you believe you have experienced in time is only a pale reflection of what is deeply hidden within you, something more real than reality itself:*

The timeless, omnipresent and omnipotent now.

It is the product of your imagination.

The world is a game of lights and shadows. When you are aware of being the author, the creator of the show and know that you are the one who is projecting it, you cannot identify yourself with it. When you are aware of this, how can a film, a show, a theatre attack you? It can only happen if you identify and if you lock yourself in this self-created prison.

To not identify with reality means to not create a division from reality; if you are the one who creates it, how can you be divided from it? If you identify, if you are trapped by your identification, you cannot enjoy your own creation.

Yesterday, you went into the world, you went to work, you met with people, you travelled, you had sex, you had fights, you laughed and you cried; what is left of it? What is left of one minute ago? Of one second ago? Only the desire to repeat, to do it again.

In order to feel enjoyment, you need to desire, to feel the absence; you need the oppositions of 'yesterday' and 'tomorrow' and you lose the now which comprehends all this, which has no polarities and no antagonisms. I am not asking you to avoid any experience; you can act in the world of events without ever losing this state of freedom from fear and doubts.

Remember! Victory and success are not in time but in some other direction. Every step you gain, every victory you win in that direction, has never to be repeated; it is there forever. Learn to think in terms of eternity. Once you have touched your inner integrity, a very powerful process of actions and events begins. Victory and freedom come to you as a natural consequence.

Your boredom asks for external reality to be renewed each time and to forget that you have created it. It calls for you to live the 'see-saw', the ups and downs, all sort of oppositions which make your life appear more real than what you see inside yourself. You think that the reflection is more real than the source; you confuse the effects with the cause, the dreamed with the Dreamer.

You must train yourself to make this revolution: the overturning of your way of seeing things, or you will be lost. To identify means to believe that what you see and touch outside is reality. It means to be the victim of concepts, descriptions and of self-hypnotism. That's why humanity needs continuous entertainment at a planetary level. It needs wars, disasters and scandals to feel occupied. But you must never forget that you are enjoying the show. That's how you can defeat death. There cannot be any suffering or pain if you know that what is called reality is nothing but a show. Start now! Or what is called 'life' will become a prison, a continuous torture.

You must train yourself to return to the now continuously. Now projects the show. Now creates all the solutions. Now contains all the joy, victory and success there is. If you are alive now, you will be alive forever.

You
Can we ever manage the flow of time?

The Dreamer
No. Time flows on and on and you, slave of nature, like a small craft, are carried away by the great current of life.

You can never manage or control the flow of time or the economics of a nation or other people's actions, because you are unable to deal with your own pain, despair and misery, and find it impossible to focus on your inner being, the only place where you can have a large measure of control over the hypnotising forces of life.

You

How can you be free of 'time', and yet still function in the everyday life? How can you go beyond time and live at the same time in a culture which is based on thought, knowledge, experience and technological achievement?

The Dreamer

The more technologically advanced you are, the more ignorant you become. You don't need anything outside of yourself. You already have everything. Self-knowledge is the only knowledge you need.

Stop believing in the external as something real and act your role in life as a great actor does on the stage. You have to ceaselessly enquire into the immeasurable and learn how to master stillness and silence while you act impeccably your role in life as an ordinary human being.

You
Everywhere around me, things are falling to pieces. How can I overcome all this?

The Dreamer
Win it before it happens!
Winning the impossible is what you're called to do.

You
But if it's already happened?

The Dreamer
Nothing can ever happen before now.
Believing to have lived through what's 'already' happened is mere imagination. It's a lie. What's 'already' happened can only happen now.
Things are not falling apart everywhere around you, but only within you. Your 'feeling' of things falling to pieces is none other than your unconquered fear still acting within you, and projecting itself into an imaginary past.
You have the presumption of having accomplished something and now you fear that this can be taken away from you. But the real tragedy is not what you perceive to be an attack on your person, your family or your business. The real tragedy is your conviction that you have a past and that the past is still there somewhere, fixed and immobile.
In reality, everything is a game. When a man curves everything he has done, everything that he believes to have conquered curves with him. In a second, he loses everything. If you depend on the past or on the imagination of the future, you are already dead!
The solution comes from inside. What happens 'outside' is only a consequence. Overcome fear and winning the impossible not only will be possible, but inevitable.

You are the only one responsible for all that happens, for all living beings, for all the good and bad in the world. There is no one in the world outside of now and no world outside of yourself.

In the Kingdom of Time, something comes first and something after.

In the infinite Kingdom of Now, nothing comes first because all and everything is happening in this very instant.

In the Kingdom of Now, you are the only living being, Creator and Sovereign of the richest, happiest and most wonderful reality.

This moment creates in all directions, 360 degrees; vastness, eternity and the infinite are only in this instant. Think what power there is; the birth of worlds, the creation of infinite generations of beings, disasters and apocalypses. All is compressed in the little eternity of this instant, in the agony of the present moment that seems to disintegrate in the past, continuously eroded, yet infinite.

You only believe in the external world and constantly fill your mind with an ocean of data: 'memories and imagination'. You believe that planning is life. When you are convinced that you did something yesterday, that something happened and you remember it, it is impossible to believe that nothing really happened and that everything is happening now, here, in this instant.

How is it possible to believe that the world is being created now, that there has never been a moment before nor after now?

The pattern you have inside made of thoughts, habits, likes and dislikes is creating your entire past and future right now. In the immensity of the moment, the past and the future are the same; one is as imaginary as the other. It is our belief system, the believing in planning, that eludes us and tricks us into thinking that we are meeting all sorts of people and doing all sorts of the things; actions that we believe to keep stored in our time-organised memory.

The illusion of being able to plan, the obstinacy of believing to be born, of having a past is the fall of divinity, the loss of omnipotence.

The moment is empty, a field in which to plant that which you desire. Plant the seed of well-being, of beauty. They will be your harvest. But for a humanity that thinks and feels negatively, it is easier to plant worrying and fear; and the world reflects and gives back weeds.

Study memory, understand that the past and future are one and the same thing, and that both are a projection of this instant; it will give you power. If you observe memory, you will set yourself free from its destructive influence.

When you don't make plans, when you don't affirm memory anymore, you gain access to intuition, to dreaming. Poetry is born. Music and art bridge between consciousness and apparent reality.

You will create new words, new expressions, new images and new life.

Conscious Suffering

You have to realise that the world with all its apparent contrasts and cruelty is only a virtual reproduction of your inner conflict and war and that outside yourself there is nothing and no one suffering but only your own self-harmfulness, sorrow and violence that take form on the set of a horror picture show.

Suffering can be useful only if it is conscious suffering.

Conscious suffering puts an end to all sufferings. Conscious suffering makes you realise that you are the solely responsible for all the troubles and difficulties that the world lives and suffers through, and at the same time, the only one who can liberate it from all evils and misery.

Remember! The world is as you dream it, and you and only you can make this world perfect by being perfect yourself.

You are here for one reason only: to win death.
Nothing else matters.
The long agony that you call reality stops existing here.

A student of inner alchemy must first develop himself within, so that through bitter practice and the bearing of disgrace, he may find the time to retreat into his own room.

What is useful, you cannot see; what is seen, cannot be used. Real treasure lies in the inner vitality, and true wealth in inner energy; this is the way to accumulate power and nourish and develop yourself within.

You must contain the world within, while attending to it without.

The task is easy, but you keep going into the world to search for tangles and complications. Sit still and grow in happiness. Accumulate your power within. Obscure your light and silence your steps, so that men have neither sight nor sound of you.

Await the hour when your fame will travel the world and be counted amongst the Immortals.

This freedom is already yours; you should only become aware of it.

Be grateful to pain and it goes. Be grateful to fear and it disappears. Be grateful to death and it will die.

Gratitude makes you whole and immortal.

Being immortal is not a human condition that you reach one day. Immortality means being in a state of aliveness now. The more you are in this state, the more you are alive. Physical immortality is a state of being! It is deathlessness!

As soon as you think of immortality, you are in a state of prosperity.

We limit ourselves to living between two poles. We are used to living in contrast but the root of all possibilities is now a state without a beginning and end.

Just putting into discussion death is an important event! History and memory breed fear. Believing in personal history doesn't give you anything; it just transforms your life into a series of painful events. Yet, it is just imagination. You feel pain in your body and live all your life in this painful state instead of deciding right now to just enjoy every second.

It's impossible to understand that you yourself create all natural disasters, but nothing comes from outside. If you understand this, it is a crime to not live in paradise.

You depend on opinions, events and circumstances as if they were real, but they are just projections of your forgetfulness. If you could live permanently in a state of integrity, how could you be attacked or find yourself in a war or earthquake, in a bankruptcy or a financial crisis?

What you are right now is creating and projecting at 360°.

Thoughtlessness, timelessness, fearlessness, deathlessness are all the same thing: inner freedom.

What do you need to remain in this state? Then do it! You'll see that everything falls into the right place and the whole world enjoys what you are living. Your disbelief in the world's description may seem like a form of cynicism, aridity, but it's not so!

You have suffered because you believe that others suffered but every man is the cause of all the human suffering that surrounds him! The world suffers because you suffer and not vice versa.

The world moulds to your every footstep; the world is a 'chewing gum' which takes the shape of your teeth!

> *'Once Narada pleaded to the Lord of the universe, "Lord, show me that Maya of Thine which can make the impossible possible." The Lord smiled and nodded in assent.*
> *Subsequently, the Lord one day set out on a journey with Narada. After going some distance, He felt very thirsty and fatigued. So, He sat down and told Narada, "Narada, I feel much thirsty; please get me a little water from somewhere."*
> *Narada at once ran in search of water.*

Finding no water nearby, he went far from the place and saw a river at a great distance. When he approached the river, he saw a most charming young lady sitting there, and was at once captivated by her beauty. As soon as Narada went near her, she began to address him in sweet words, and soon, both fell in love with each other.
Narada then married her, and settled down as a householder.
In course of time, he had a number of children by her.
And while he was thus living happily with his wife and children, there came a plague in the country. Death began to collect its toll from every place. Then Narada proposed to abandon the place and go somewhere else. His wife agreed to it, and they both came out of their house leading their children by the hand.
But no sooner did they come to the bridge to cross the river than there came a terrible flood, and in the rush of water, all their children were swept away one after another, and at last the wife too was drowned.
Overwhelmed with grief at his bereavement, Narada sat down on the bank and began to weep piteously. Just then, the Lord appeared before him, saying, "O Narada, where is the water you were going to bring me? And why are you weeping?" The sight of the Lord startled the sage, and then he understood everything. He exclaimed, "Lord, my obeisance to Thee, and my obeisance also to thy wonderful Maya!"'

—From *The Gospel of Sri Ramakrishna*

As told in the ancient story of Narada, the material world can transform into something hostile and violent, for he who indulges in sleep, for he who has forgotten his dream.

This is important to understand. You can do very much for humanity if you get rid of the rubbish you carry within yourself and simply *remember*.

It is in this precise moment that you can do something, and it is always in this precise moment! Right now, you can liberate the world from all the tribulations and sufferings and guilt you have been subject to all your life.

Every man is a victim of his own self; as soon as an atom of fear, a doubt comes within, you have to circumscribe it. You have to be free from your guilt and suffering. A paradise on earth—a portable paradise depends only on you in this moment. Pierce all the outer layers to enter into your buried will, and see that there is endless wealth and abundance.

When the will does not work, accidentality
takes over, and human disasters and gloomy
events are the inevitable outcome

If you don't regain your role as creator, you will be out of the game forever. Fires, disease and accidents will be your welcome visitors as you search desperately for excuses to justify your lack of happiness and success.

Take on the problems of the entire world! Ask the universe to invest in you, to entrust its entire weight to you, as if you have been schooled by Atlas himself. Wherever you go, the world will receive pleasure, understanding, joy of life because your being will contain all things.

Take five minutes for yourself! Whether you feel good or not, just stay there and watch. Don't waste time! The observer, to the observed, is God.

Healing the scars inside means seeing the stars outside. When you've learned to look inside yourself and dissolve the 'problem', you've 'made it'. Real doing is just this 'not doing'.

When pain comes inside, your conscious absence permits the world to reflect that absence and go beyond. As soon as you've taken charge of that space or of that event, that disaster disappears.

When you are present, you master the game and contain the universe. That is the real victory.

Healing the 'scars' reveals the 'stars'.

The Kingdom of Now

If you focus on the 'now', time will be no longer linear but simultaneous; past, present and future will co-exist.

In this frame of 'conscious awareness', you create the New World: new types of light-based technologies, new ways of communication, new forms of community-living, new forms of government, new resources, new economy, new financial and educational systems, and all overwhelmed by joy, harmony and beauty.

In a state of timelessness, any achievement or understanding will cease to have any meaning, and whatever you have held as sacred or important, no longer will have any significance for you. Here is the crucial point where something higher, deeper, greater has to take place. And this can only happen from within yourself, in absence of time.

The Fairy-tale of Your Own Birth and Death

You

You said that birth and death are just descriptions, concepts, false beliefs and that life doesn't come from our parents but stands real, eternal, magnificent, with neither beginning nor ending. I have witnessed two great happenings in the last few months which have deeply marked my life: the birth of my son and the death of my mother.

Do you think I was just imagining all that?

The Dreamer

What you have witnessed with your own eyes is none other than the fairy-tale of your own birth and death that nobody else, but you yourself, in this precise instant, are producing and projecting on the imaginary picture screen that you call 'reality'.

Death is the end of an imaginary life,
eternal life is the end of an imaginary death.

Only you, living permanently in the 'here now' can liberate the world from all opposites.

Only you, abandoning your inner conflict, will free the world from all contradictions, violence and wars. 'The crack between conflicting opposites is the gateway to immortality'.

The idea of immortality doesn't need you to believe, because what you really are, you can only be.

Believing makes you doubt your very being. Becoming immortal is a false idea. You cannot become what you already are. You have to work so much on the false idea that one day you are going to die to realise that death is only an imaginary belief that you have imposed on your life.

An inner sense of immortality is needed to overcome all limits and boundaries that the world imposes on you. The idea that death is inevitable is the very cause of all failure, disease and ultimately death itself.

Remember! Once won the war with time, there will be no more wars to fight.

If you apply timelessness to what is in time or governed by time, victory over death will be the natural result. In timelessness, you live and project your reality from a gravitational centre entirely different than that of the ordinary man, commanding events and moulding time itself at your service.

The more time you spend in timeless silence, the more 'time' will be given to you. You will understand that beliefs, hopes and expectations, plans, imaginations and desires are all children of time, and as such, they are false and very harmful.

Remember! Timelessness is a practical technology.

The world lasts but for an instant—this instant. It's only your time memory that makes you think that the world continues.

Don't live by memory! Memory is a liar. Time is a liar!
'Past is dust'.

See the world as it is: a simultaneous creation of your inner being that, according to your inner states and conditions, appears and disappears at will and can become something alien and violent if you forget that you yourself are the very source of its existence.

Time has to serve. Time is to be used. Time wants to be governed. Time is a creature of the timeless you, devoted to express, in the world of events, your creativity, your inner silence, your eternity.

The choice is ultimately up to you. The choice is time or timelessness, pleasure or misery, life forever or death.

Tear apart the veil of time to allow your disintegrated being to *remember*, to put together the scattered limbs and, for a few moments, savour immortality.

Man is a decayed being, a god fallen into a state of amnesia, a god who has forgotten the power of creativity.

Think about what powers man has, and how he could put them at the service of the world. Power of dreaming, power of thinking, power of feeling, seeing and touching—power of will, power of breathing, aspiring and healing.

> *Man is a self-fulfilling god.*
> *Man is a self-realising god.*
> *Man is a self-loving god.*
> *Man is a self-responsible god.*
> *Man is a death-winning god.*
> *Man is earth-transforming god.*
> *Man possesses within himself the source of all truth, good and beauty.*

Creative powers that only a conscious being can possess. Being aware means to remember—means to get out of a state of amnesia and remember whom you really are: an infinite permanent, unborn and immortal being.

You
Can I ever become you one day?

The Dreamer
You are already me: life without birth and without death.

Live fearlessly, and there is nothing you cannot conquer.
Live thoughtlessly, and you will realise all that you have desired and dreamed of.

Live timelessly, and you will taste what man has searched for so long and never found:

Everlasting Life.

*Dream the impossible, and it will instantly appear before you.
Dream! It is your dreaming which creates and projects the incredible world you are living in.*